FAST BREAK

HEROES OF THE NBA

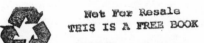

FAST BREAK

HEROES OF THE NBA

Kevin McHale, Julius Erving,
Bobby Jones, Mark Eaton,
Marques Johnson, Butch Carter,
Kiki Vandeweghe, and others...

AL JANSSEN

Here's Life Publishers

Published by
HERE'S LIFE PUBLISHERS, INC.
P.O. Box 1576
San Bernardino, CA 92402

HLP Product No. 951574

Library of Congress Cataloging-in-Publication Data
Janssen, Al.
    Fast break.

    1. Basketball players — United States — Biography.
2. National Basketball Association.   3. Sports — Religious
aspects — Christianity.   I. Title.
GV884.A1J36   1987   796.32'3'0922   [B]   86-22771
ISBN 0-89840-134-8 (pbk.)

Cover photo courtesy of the Bosten Celtics, © 1986 by Dick Raphael
Associates

Scripture quotations are from the New American Standard Bible,
© The Lockman Foundation 1960, 1962, 1963, 1968, 1971, 1972,
1973, 1975, and are used by permission.

For More Information, Write:

L.I.F.E. — P.O. Box A399, Sydney South 2000, Australia

Campus Crusade for Christ of Canada — Box 300, Vancouver, B.C. V6C 2X3, Canada
Campus Crusade for Christ — 103 Friar Street, Reading RG1 1EP, Berkshire, England
Lay Institute for Evangelism — P.O. Box 8786, Auckland 3, New Zealand
Great Commission Movement of Nigeria — P.O. Box 500, Jos, Plateau State Nigeria, West Africa
Campus Crusade for Christ International — Arrowhead Springs, San Bernardino, CA 92414, U.S.A.

To my dear wife
JO
who endured many lonely nights
so that this book could be written
and
my two precious sons
JOSHUA and JONATHAN

Contents

1

FUN TIME IN DALLAS

A jam-packed crowd at the Reunion Arena in Dallas had clapped, yelled, stomped, and cheered for nearly two hours. This was everything they'd ever hoped for in a basketball game. The NBA's finest players were putting on a show worthy of the All-Star game.

From the opening seconds when Earvin "Magic" Johnson of the Lakers had lobbed a pass to Houston's 7'4" Ralph Sampson for a backboard-rattling slam dunk, these stars had attempted to out-do each other with spectacular passes, blistering fast breaks, daring drives, precision shooting, muscle-flexing rebounds, and surprise steals.

It was now midway through the third quarter and for the past four minutes, the two teams had traded the lead ten times. It was a tense moment as fans and players waited to see which team would assume control.

A three-point field goal by Milwaukee's Sidney Moncrief gave the East team a two-point lead. It was the West's turn to counter. Rolando Blackman of the Dallas Mavericks rushed the ball up court. At the top of the key, he saw an opening and drove into the lane. Boston's Kevin McHale and Atlanta's Dominique Wilkins quickly blocked his path. In mid-air, Blackman attempted to shoot over the imposing wall. With a flick of his wrist, McHale deflected the ball to Detroit guard Isiah Thomas at the free throw line.

Instantly, Wilkins began a dash down the left side, with Moncrief on the far right and Larry Bird in the middle. Thomas took one quick dribble and shot-putted a pass to Wilkins. The only West defender against this three-on-one break was San Antonio's Alvin Robertson, who quickly moved to cut off Wilkins' drive and force a pass. But Wilkins had a better idea. As he took off from the left corner of the free throw line, he spun around 360 degrees to avoid Robertson and neatly laid the ball into the basket. Seconds later, Moncrief scored another layup to give the East a six-point lead and West coach Pat Riley of the Lakers was calling for a time-out to regroup his forces.

It was just one stunning moment in a game filled with eye-popping plays. The West would rally again, only to fall to the East in the final moments, 139-132. This one play, however, demonstrated teamwork in harmony with incredible individual athletic skills, for the fast break is indeed the epitome of both elements. Everyone has a job to do, beginning on defense with pressure on the ball and position under the boards; to the instant of transition when the ball is gained through rebound or steal; to the race down the court as every player fills a lane, probing for the opening or mismatch that will lead to an easy layup.

Isiah Thomas admitted that directing a fast break in the All-Star game is "like heaven. You come down on the court and you have 'Dr. J' on your right and Larry Bird on your left. If you pass it to Doc it's right, and if you pass it to Larry it's right. And if you pass it to the trailer, that's right, too!"

The beauty of the fast break is that everyone can participate, from the giant center to the smallest guard. And on this showcase All-Star weekend in Dallas, these NBA players demonstrated that basketball is a game everyone can enjoy. For while fans were awed by the size and skill of eleven giants who stood 6'9" and taller, including six at 7' or more, the favorites were two little men who stole the show.

One afternoon earlier, Spud Webb of the Atlanta Hawks — at 5'7" a full ten inches shorter than the

next-smallest competitor — leaped, whirled, and jammed his way to the NBA slam dunk championship.
Then Sunday afternoon, 6'1" Isiah Thomas led both
teams with 30 points, dished off 10 assists, made 5
steals, and even grabbed a rebound to earn unanimous
selection as the game's most valuable player. Spud and
Isiah had demonstrated again why basketball has become one of the world's favorite sports. And the most fun.

During All-Star weekend, numerous events made
one fact clear: Basketball is so much fun to these men
that if they were not paid huge salaries, they'd be out
on a cement driveway or an asphalt playground — just
shooting, or playing one-on-one, two-on-two, Horse, or
a half-court pick-up game.

Nineteen NBA old-timers, ranging in age from thirty-
eight to sixty, showed that they still enjoyed the game
with a nostalgic reunion before the slam dunk competition. Former greats like Dave Cowens, Bob Cousy,
John Havlicek, Nate Thurmond, Oscar Robertson, Connie Hawkins, and Elvin Hayes huffed and puffed up
and down the court, playing with a competitive intensity
that amazed everyone. "I felt like a rookie in this game,"
said 5'9" Calvin Murphy, who survived thirteen years
in the league, all with the Houston Rockets. "At times
I felt like getting some autographs."

Fun was also evident in the competition to determine
who was basketball's most accurate long-distance shooter. Eight of the NBA's most accurate three-point shooters
decided to find out. Larry Bird demonstrated his great-
ness in the final round by making 11 straight shots and

18 out of 25 to win. "I'm the three-point king!" he exulted. It was almost as if the superstar enjoyed this more than winning his third straight league MVP crown.

Other fun-filled moments were more spontaneous. After the East team's practice, Kevin McHale and Isiah Thomas tried to see who could make the craziest shots in an impromptu game of Horse. They took shots from mid-court, from behind the backboard, spread-legged across the baseline, and from beyond the sidelines. Their grins convinced everyone that no matter who won, both had enjoyed the contest.

It was also a time for one of the league's superstars to announce that he wasn't finished having fun playing against the best in basketball. Following the game in the winning East locker room, Julius Erving sat in front of his locker, his legs stretched out on another chair as his aching knees were blanketed with large bags of ice. A horde of reporters crowded around as the future Hall-of-Famer announced that after fifteen years of pro basketball, he wasn't ready to call it quits.

"When did you make the decision?" one reporter asked.

"Last Monday. I've been thinking about it for some time and I decided this was just what I wanted to do every day next year."

"What convinced you that you wanted to come back?"

"Physically I knew I could dedicate myself. Spiritually, I was at peace that this was where God wanted me to be. Emotionally, I was divided. I like being home and seeing my kids every day. But overall, the pluses outweighed the minuses."

One reporter noted that the fans had voted him a starter in the All-Star game for the tenth straight year. "Did you draw any input from the fans?"

"I got a lot of fan mail. There were a lot of letters that went into detail why they thought I should continue to play. I didn't get any letters saying I should hang them up after this year."

So basketball fans could breath a sigh of relief that The Doctor, who had given them so many incredible thrills, would be around for another year to provide a few more of his original moves.

In the midst of this fun-filled weekend, there were other NBA players who also allowed some time for contemplation. Before the 1986 All-Stars took the court for their annual show, several of them gathered along with other guests of the league for a special chapel service. Rolando Blackman introduced the program, explaining that the guests were having a rare opportunity. "Chapel is a time when we get away for a few minutes and reflect on what's really important in life."

During the service, 7'2" Artis Gilmore, a man many consider one of the strongest in the NBA, shared how he was not strong enough to cope with life's trials alone. Before reading a section from Psalms in the Bible, he said, "I remember going down with a knee injury in Chicago, and another time when I suffered a blow to the head and broke three bones. Both times I thought my career was over. The fact that I'm still playing is because of the Lord. I can say with the Psalm writer that I will praise the Lord, no matter what happens. I will boast of all His kindness to me."

Alex English, at that moment the NBA's leading scorer, listened and understood. Twelve months earlier, he'd made headlines by persuading his fellow All-Stars to donate their All-Star game checks to famine relief in Ethiopia. It was an expression of faith built as a child under the teaching of his grandmother. "Basketball is my art," he said, "a way of expression. But when you look at it on the overall scale of the world, it's such a minute thing. I owe everything to God, and that was one way I could give a little back to Him."

Dr. J, Rolando, Artis, and Alex are not unique in this league. Many players have discovered that basketball is a fun, challenging and a great way to earn a living — but that there is far more to life. In the next few chapters, you will meet several of these men. Some of them are perennial All-Stars, like Kevin McHale, Terry Cummings, Bobby Jones, and Marques Johnson. Others like Kelvin Ransey, Gene banks, and A.C. Green are not household names. But each of them has an important story to tell.

Each of these players can run a fast break. They know how to acquire the ball, make the transition, and push for a slam dunk after a well-orchestrated dash down the court. Each of them has also experienced a spiritual fast break, a moment when they made the transition ˙from living for themselves and the world to a life committed to God. That commitment has had a wide variety of implications. It's helped one to conquer drug abuse, another to overcome near financial ruin, a third to maximize his academic potential, and still another to prepare for his life's work after basketball.

You may also find some unusual perspectives in these chapters. You'll go into the referees' locker room and see how officials prepare to work an NBA game. You'll attend a pre-game chapel service with the Portland Trail Blazers. You'll discover how an NBA rookie adjusts to life in the pros while living out of a suitcase for several months.

So sit back, relax, and enjoy a visit with some of the heroes of the NBA. Let them take you behind the scenes, give a few insights into this great game, and share some of the lessons they've learned about life. They'll admit they don't have all of the answers, and they certainly aren't perfect. But they have found a spiritual dimension that gives life meaning on and off the court.

Let's begin at the place where many an NBA season has concluded . . . the Boston Garden.

Kevin McHale

2

IT'S ALL
IN THE FAMILY
Kevin McHale

There is a mystique about the Boston Celtics. It's reflected in the sixteen world championship banners hanging from the rafters of the Boston Garden. It includes the unique parquet floor in that same arena, invoking the memory of great Celtics teams of the past that won eleven NBA titles between 1957 and 1969. It's contained in the two additional banners bearing fifteen retired numbers of past Celtics stars — men such as Bill Russell,

Bob Cousy, John Havlicek, Sam and K.C. Jones, and Dave Cowens.

Much of the mystique resides in the Celtics' patriarch, team president Red Auerbach. He coached nine of the championship teams himself, and masterminded the trades and drafts that put these and other title winners together.

In all of those years, the Celtics never had an NBA scoring champion. Rather, Auerbach assembled talent that fit his total team concept. Other NBA teams might have equal or even greater individual talent, but the Celtics have won more games than any other NBA team in history.

Kevin McHale fits the Celtics mold. He's not blessed with exceptional athletic skills (his coach, K.C. Jones, says, "He can't outrun a turtle"), but he makes up for it with scrappy and intelligent play, and with versatility. He's excelled at the power forward and center positions, both as a starter and as a sixth man. He gives his team scoring, defense, and rebounding. It's been good enough to win him two "Sixth Man" awards and two selections to the NBA All-Star game.

"There are a lot of things I like about him," said Auerbach during the 1985 playoffs. "But the thing I like most of all is that he's like (Larry) Bird in that he'll play hurt. . . . He loves to play, and shows up motivated almost every single night."

That recognition from the number one Celtic came during one of the few times the Boston mystique failed.

Eight times since 1959 the Celts had defeated the Los Angeles Lakers franchise in the championship series, and they had never lost the NBA title while playing on their home court. Both of those incredible streaks ended on June 9, 1985. Ironically, it was on that date that Kevin McHale was finally recognized as one of the league's premiere players.

The previous year, the Celtics had won their fifteenth title in a scintillating seven games with the Lakers. McHale's stats weren't spectacular, but many feel he made the pivotal play of the series. It happened in game four with Boston down two games to one. Kurt Rambis broke away on a fast break and Kevin, in the process of preventing the score, sent the Laker forward flying. From then on, the Celtics wore down L.A. with their more physical play.

The Lakers fought back with some physical play of their own in the '85 series. McHale insists that his Celtics could have won that series with a healthy Larry Bird. The league's MVP that season was suffering from bone chips in his right elbow and a jammed right index finger and was unable to perform at his normally incredible level. Kevin tried to take up the slack. He led both teams with an average of 26 points and 10 rebounds during the six-game series, and in the final game, he almost single-handedly kept the Celtics in contention. Before fouling out with five-and-a-half minutes to play, he scored 32 points and pulled down 16 rebounds. After he left, the Lakers pulled away to a 111-100 triumph.

In the 1986 championship series against Houston, Kevin again led both teams in scoring, but this time the Celts also had a healthy and inspired Larry Bird and backup center Bill Walton. The result was title number sixteen, and some were calling this team one of the greatest ever. With Walton supporting center Robert Parish, Kevin could finally concentrate on one position, and he was rapidly earning a reputation as one of the NBA's top power forwards.

Boston coach K.C. Jones acknowledged that with the 6'10" McHale in his starting lineup, opponents have problems. "He causes beautiful mismatches," said Jones about teaming Kevin, 7' center Robert Parish, and of course, Bird. "It allows Larry to be the small forward. Teams have difficulty dealing with that front line."

Hubie Brown, coach of the New York Knicks, agreed: "The primary problem McHale presents is his size. He's bigger than the majority of the people he plays against. Add his long arms and he is a classic postup player with an abundance of offensive moves. His fadeaway jumper is impossible to stop."

For several years, Kevin was the latest in a storied line of Celtic sixth men such as Frank Ramsey and John Havlicek who could come off the bench and infuse the team with quick offense or tenacious defense. In 1984 and 1985 Kevin won the NBA Sixth Man Award before he became even more useful as a starter.

"It doesn't matter whether I start or come off the bench," Kevin said after he became a starter. "My overriding concern is winning." Yet there is a difference in the two roles. "When you're the sixth man, you get to study the play, see what needs to be done, and then go in and concentrate on the areas we might be lacking. As a starter, you don't have the luxury of finding out what has to be emphasized.

It's Kevin's adaptability that makes him so valuable. Besides his height, his unusually long arms make him a formidable shot blocker. He has a deadly hook shot and can fill the basket in a hurry. During one hot streak in March of 1985, he had consecutive games of 56 and 42 points. The 98 points for two games set a team record. And, according to Jones, "He's a scrapper. He does the best he can with the abilities he has."

Kevin's scrappy style of play has its roots in the midwest, specifically Hibbing, Minnesota, a mining town of 21,000 people. His father worked for years in the open pit iron ore mines, and raised two boys. Kevin was a typical kid who fought with his brother, competed in sports, and enjoyed the rural lifestyle.

The competition with his brother, Paul, had a lot to do with his success in basketball. "I'm sure we drove my parents crazy," he says. "We challenged each other to get better at everything we did because neither of us wanted to lose to the other. In the negative sense, we argued too much. But in a positive way we learned that competition can be very healthy when you're striving to do your best and improve."

Kevin speaks fondly of his father. "We had a great relationship. He did a lot of shift work, so sometimes we didn't see him that much. But he was someone I could always talk to. His children and his wife were his life. He never shoved anything down our throats. The only thing he made us do was go to church every Sunday."

Kevin owns a home in Hibbing and every summer, with his wife and two children, he escapes from Boston and returns to the simple life. "This is where I feel really comfortable," he explains. He spends the summer hunting and fishing and enjoying his hard-working, down-to-earth friends and neighbors.

Family is extremely important to this man with traditional, midwestern values. His wife, Lynn, is also a Hibbing native and they dated for several years. "I took my time getting married," he laughs, "but we got to know each other really well. She's a very good person, but she's also very strong in a lot of ways. We draw a lot from each other. She gives me stability. I've learned through her that you have to sacrifice, compromise and be willing to change."

But it took some time for Kevin to learn how to make those changes. When the couple's first child, Kristen, was born, Lynn shouldered the load of raising her while Kevin acted as if nothing was different. "All of a sudden, one day I woke up," he explains. "I realized that Lynn had all of the responsibility. I needed to pitch in and help. When I did, I found out how much fun it is to be around our kids."

An important element in this family is their faith. While Kevin was required to attend church as a boy, it wasn't until he was at the University of Minnesota that he began learning what it meant to be a Christian.

Kevin was one of three players on the Minnesota Gophers basketball team who participated in a regular Bible study. Andy Thompson was another member of that threesome. "The Bible studies were open to anyone on the team after dinner but most of the guys went back to their rooms," says Andy, now an art dealer in Oregon following a pro basketball career in Europe. "I was encouraged that Kevin came because it meant someone else on the team shared the same interest and motivation I did. However, I'll admit neither of us was very strong spiritually."

The studies covered topics such as dating, sex, giving your best in sports and school, and being totally committed to Christ. With that biblical perspective, Kevin began understanding all the sermons he'd heard as a boy. "I realized that there's a lot more to life than shooting jump shots and getting rebounds, or trying to get A's and B's in school. That's all very important, but life has more meaning than that. I became really interested in the teaching of Jesus, and the fact that He died for my sins. It all began to make sense, and I decided to believe it and try to live by it.

"I think the main thing it affected was my priorities. I realized what's important and what's not. Putting that into practice is hard, because you've done a lot of wrong things all your life and the habits are hard to break."

One thing people notice about Kevin is that he laughs easily and throws himself wholeheartedly into whatever he does. "I've never felt that being a Christian means you have to be a sourpuss," he explains. "I have a beautiful family and a great job. How can I not be happy?"

Andy says that in college Kevin was never serious about anything. "If someone scored 35 points over him, he'd come back to the locker room, be quiet for three or four minutes, then toss it off with a joke. He was a happy-go-lucky guy. He still likes to have a good time, but his priorities have changed."

Many players complain about the constant travel required in the NBA. Most agree it's the one thing they won't miss after their careers. It's particularly hard on a family man. The wife is stuck at home with the kids for up to two weeks at a time. And the children don't understand why Daddy has to be gone. Phone bills can get exorbitant as the players try to stay in touch with home.

Occasionally Kevin has found the needs of his family in conflict with his Celtics family. When Boston was scheduled to play on national television in New York on Christmas Day, 1985, league rules required them to be in the city the night before. Even though Boston is a short plane ride to New York, there are no exceptions to this rule, even for the holidays. However, the league offered to pay for the families to join the players on this trip.

Kevin McHale didn't like the idea. He thought of all his Christmases as a kid, the special family togetherness, the tree and opening presents together. "I sure didn't want to wake up in a hotel room on Christmas morning and I felt it was totally wrong for my kids. When I told the team, they were upset. But my family comes before basketball."

Kevin flew to New York Christmas Day in plenty of time for the game. "I would never miss a game. That's hard to justify because they pay me very good money. I have a responsibility. They asked me if I had come down the night before. I could have lied, but I knew that wasn't right." When he told them the truth, he was ordered to pay a fine. "It was well worth it," he concludes.

Andy Thompson thinks that example demonstrates the maturity Kevin has gained since his college days. Having experienced his own spiritual renewal while playing pro basketball in France, Andy's priorities have also changed. He told about meeting Kevin recently in Minnesota and having a long talk with him over breakfast: "Kevin admitted that after he turned pro he had done some things he shouldn't have because he was living only for himself. When he realized that wasn't what God had planned for him, he settled down and turned into a good family man who puts God first. That was a real encouragement to me."

The Celtics family is committed to putting together championship teams that will add to their collection of banners in the Boston Garden. Kevin is dedicated to helping achieve that goal. But when pro basketball is over, Kevin McHale will still have his wife and kids. He's even more committed to investing time and energy in that family, which will remain long after the memory of his basketball accomplishments has faded.

A. C. Green

3

NEW LIFE
IN THE PROS
A. C. Green

The home of A. C. Green, Sr., and his wife is a tidy blue ranch-style structure in northeast Portland, just a few blocks from the Columbia River. As I entered the front door, a full-length painting of the Greens' youngest child, dressed in the gold and purple uniform of the Los Angeles Lakers, greeted me.

To the left of the entryway, on top of a stereo cabinet, sat several trophies, including a large silver number 1 symbolizing outstanding high school sports performance. Beside it was a picture of football great O.J. Simpson presenting the award to a tall young man on behalf of the Hertz Corporation.

The proud mother and father escorted me through the kitchen-dining area into the family room. Here the four walls made up a Hall-of-Fame-type display of plaques, newspaper clippings and photographs. A poster promoting the Far-West Classic basketball tournament featured a tuxedo-clad member of the Green family dunking a basketball. An Oregon daily sports page headlined, "Praise the Lord and Pass the Ball." A collage of photos, matted with the bright orange of Oregon State University, featured memorable snapshots of the family basketball star from preschool through college graduation. And featured over the display was a picture of Jesus Christ. "Junior wanted Him to be above all of this," Mrs. Green explained.

"Junior" is better known as A. C. Green, who is in the early stages of his NBA career. As a reserve forward, he was helping the Los Angeles Lakers by hustling every second of an average 19 minutes per game, crashing the boards, playing tough defense, and scoring eight points per game. Lakers coach Pat Riley had paid the supreme compliment to his number one draft choice: "There's only one other player I've seen come into this league in the last six years who has his awareness and perception. And that was Earvin." Yes, Riley was comparing Green to his superstar guard, Earvin "Magic" Johnson.

The first thing fans want to know about Green is what the initials "A. C." stand for. His older siblings have conventional names — Lee, Vanessa, and Steve. But the youngest is always called "Junior" by his mother. "I named him A. C. because he looked so much like his father," she said as we talked in the living room.

The son himself had admitted earlier that he didn't know what the letters stood for. "Let me know if you find out," he laughed. So I asked his father. A. C. Sr. was silent for a moment, staring out the living room window. Perhaps this great mystery would finally be solved. Then he shook his head and said, "Nah, it don't mean nothin'."

The family's star basketball player had been home only three times in the past four months, twice when the Lakers visited the Memorial Coliseum a few miles to the south, the other for a very brief Christmas break. This was the first extended time Junior had spent away from his family, and it was perhaps his hardest adjustment to professional basketball. He tried to compensate by talking to family members by phone, sometimes two or three times a day. "Junior has always been family oriented," his mother said. "He never was into street life. He was the quiet one and he didn't want to disappoint us."

*   *   *

One thousand miles south of the comforts of home, A. C. met me at the Airport Park Hotel. It was mid-December, and the temperature had soared into the 70s.

The hotel was A. C.'s temporary home, parked between the Fabulous Forum on the north and Hollywood Park racetrack on the south.

He was dressed in an Avia T-shirt and shiny black sweat pants. The previous night, A. C. had scored 17 points in a losing cause at Denver. The team had just landed in Los Angeles an hour earlier and Green was using a few free moments to catch up on laundry. Later he planned to go apartment hunting, then meet with his agent. Tomorrow there was a game against Detroit, then early Monday morning the team would fly to New York to begin a four-game road trip.

We entered Champs, a bright and cheerful coffee shop in the hotel lobby. All the waitresses and bus boys knew the Lakers rookie. "I've got the menu memorized," he laughed. With the Forum in use approximately 300 days a year, many athletes and performers use this hotel. Two members of the Washington Capitals hockey team were grabbing a pre-game bite, while in the back, a solemn group of young men, dressed in drab charcoal-gray suits, occupied several tables. They were members of a Soviet hockey team that would play the NHL Kings in a couple of days.

As we sat by the window and watched the cars stream into the south parking lot for the afternoon racing program, A. C. admitted he was tired of hotel life. "I'm ready to move into my own place and have my own bedroom, my own refrigerator, my own food, and cook any time I want to. But I haven't found the place I really want. My prayer is that I'll have a place before Christmas."

A. C. admitted that life in Los Angeles was a far cry from home. "The quiet times here are like the busiest times in Portland." And the people? Well, he'd met a lot of interesting characters. "I'm finding out there are some places you have to stay away from if you want to keep your integrity and morality. So many people want to be associated with Lakers players. Ladies are always coming up to you or trying to call you. You really have to use discretion as to who you hang around with."

Since his junior year at Oregon State University when he was PAC-10 Player of the Year, A. C. had trained for the opportunity to play pro basketball. He'd put himself on a weightlifting program to improve his strength and endurance, and had worked to increase his shooting ability.

The primary adjustment as a pro was the number of games. "In college, it's pressure packed; nearly every game is vital," A. C. commented. "In the NBA, you go out on the court more relaxed because you know there's another game tomorrow. The hardest part is being consistent — trying to get your rebounds every night, even when you're physically tired or you're not mentally into the game. That's a challenge."

While few experts doubted A. C.'s basketball ability, there were questions about his lifestyle. It was rumored that several teams had passed by him in the draft because he chanted and had other unusual religious practices. While it is true that Green has deep convictions, it doesn't take one long to realize that he is a normal person, with an extraordinary love for God.

That's a dramatic change from his teenage years when he was more concerned about being accepted by his friends. The peer pressure didn't lead to drug or alcohol abuse or sexual immorality, for it was counter-balanced by a strong family environment. But, A. C. admits, "One of my things was cursing. I would never do it at home, but I did it at school. I was always laughing and joking and playing around. The reason I even played basketball was to be accepted."

It's almost shocking when Green states, "I've only had an alcoholic beverage one time and smoked one time. And I've never slept with a girl." Yet he frankly admits that he was "definitely living in sin. I wasn't doing anything according to God's law."

It might be said he had a good excuse — he didn't know very much about God and His law. The family did attend church until Green reached his teenage years, but he stopped because few of his friends attended church. Then, just a couple of months before he headed to Oregon State University, Green and several of his friends decided to take a weekend trip across Oregon to visit one of their former teachers — Rod Bragado. It was a life-changing weekend.

The four-hour drive took them to Hermiston, a small town on the Columbia River in eastern Oregon. A. C. seemed to enjoy reliving that moment as he told the story. "The Sunday before we headed home, we all went to church. I told Rod I didn't have any appropriate clothes to wear, and he said to just wear what we had on. So we went in our jeans and T-shirts. I don't know how many blacks they had in Hermiston but there weren't very many. And there weren't any at this church. There were about 150 people, and Rod took us ten black kids up front, to the second row.

"I'll never forget the sermon. It was called, 'Do You Want to Go to Heaven or Hell?' To understand why this particular sermon meant so much to me, you have to understand that until then — I was seventeen years old — all I knew about Jesus was His name. I didn't know His mother was Mary. I didn't know He was the Son of God. I didn't have any knowledge of who Jesus was. In Sunday school I'd heard He died on a cross, but that was it.

"My lifestyle was based on this reasoning: If I could be a good person, obey my parents and not do anything they would be ashamed of, then I would go to heaven. However, if I did my own thing — drank, smoke, slept around, didn't obey my parents — then I would go to hell. That was A. C. Green's bible.

"The reason the sermon was so dynamic for me was that I finally heard God's version of the Bible. I learned about obeying God's laws, and what I had to do to enter His kingdom. God said the way I went to heaven was by believing in His Son Jesus Christ, who died on the cross for my sins and then rose from the dead.

"When the preacher finished his sermon, he invited anyone who wanted to accept Jesus as their Lord and Savior to come forward. My best friend was sitting to my right, by the aisle, It was easy access to the front. But I thought, *My friends are going to laugh at me if I go.*

"The second time the pastor made the invitation — 'Would anyone here like to accept Jesus?' — I said in my heart, *Yes, I would.* Now I was sweating. I nudged my friend to see if he'd go first. But he didn't. I wanted to go, but I didn't want to go alone. The pastor repeated his invitation twice and finally I said, 'I'm going.' I stepped over my friend and into the aisle. Although only one row separated me from the altar, that was the longest walk I've ever taken. It seemed like walking down a long tunnel.

"When I finally reached the pastor, he said, 'Young man, do you know what you're doing?' I said, 'No, not totally, but I know I want to go to heaven.' So we prayed and I believed and asked Jesus Christ to come into my life. When we finished, the pastor told me to turn around. I turned and all my friends were clapping!

"That's the most important day of my life. August 2, 1981. The day I was born again."

*   *   *

Leon Jordan is an intense young man. On this particular Saturday morning, he was in the midst of an all-day study session as he prepared for the California Bar exam. During a break he talked about his work as A. C. Green's agent.

Jordan played basketball at Oregon State University in the mid-1970s, then attended law school at the University of Oregon. After earning his law degree, he went to work for a large accounting firm in Portland. One of his clients was Mychal Thompson, a member of the Portland Trail Blazers who had run into financial difficulty because of fraudulent investments by his agent. Jordan helped Mychal resolve some of his problems, which eventually landed the original agent in jail. That motivated Jordan to begin helping other professional athletes.

About A. C. Green, Jordan said, "He is very good hearted, and has a true commitment to the Lord, which is very unusual. I almost felt a burden for him because people saw him as perfect. I was concerned about the pressure he was under, but so far he's handled it very well. He was also very young in the sense of business." That's why Green, after retaining Jordan as his agent, sat in on all the contract negotiations with the Lakers. "We were a team," Jordan explained of the unusual procedure.

Jordan's function was to handle contract negotiations, then arrange Green's financial affairs so A. C. could concentrate on playing basketball. The negotiations were difficult. The Lakers' first offer was a one-year contract at the minimum salary of $75,000. Their explanation sounded logical; the team was above the league's salary cap.

Perhaps the team also thought they were dealing with amateurs from the backwoods of Oregon. But Leon Jordan had done his homework. He knew that there were twenty-one exceptions to the league's salary cap rules. He also knew what other late first-round draft choices were being paid. He informed the Lakers that they had to make some decisions. "The team has to be loyal to people who have helped them in the past," Leon explained, "but they also have to plan for the future."

Neither Green nor Jordan expected the backlash after they rejected the Lakers' first offer. Leon received as many as ten calls per day from fans who told him he was ruining his client's life. "I got a call from a little old lady in Los Angeles who told me I should be ashamed. That was hard as a Christian businessman. I had to question, 'Am I being greedy?' However, I also had to do what was right for my client. I perceived that we needed to gain the team's respect in order to lay a foundation for future negotiations." Plans were made for Green to play ball in Europe if an agreement wasn't reached.

The Lakers broke the stalemate by releasing two highly paid free agents — Bob McAdoo and Jamaal Wilkes. Under salary cap rules, half of those salaries could be applied to a new player. Shortly before training camp opened, the Lakers and Green agreed to a four-year contract valued at about $800,000. "We made the right decision," Jordan said.

*   *   *

It was another city, another hotel. A. C. Green knew he was at the Northfield Hilton, somewhere outside Detroit. Fog obscured the view outside the window, and a light snow had fallen during the night. He remembered the team landing at night, and a long bus ride to the hotel during which he tried to sleep. "I don't know which direction we took or anything."

It was mid-January and the next day the Lakers would face the Detroit Pistons on national television. As he stretched out on his bed, Green said he finally had a home. "I got an apartment on Christmas Eve. It's about twenty minutes from the Forum." He also confessed he was finding it hard to navigate around the city. "This past week, I got lost every day. I'd make a decision on a turn and find out, sometimes twenty minutes later, that I'd made the wrong turn. Driving in L.A. has been quite an experience."

Concerning the contract negotiations and the criticism he and Jordan received, Green admitted that it was a pressure-packed time. "I tried to keep my perspective and not let the negotiations dictate how I felt and acted." He disagreed with those who criticized him for not accepting the minimum salary. "I believe Christians should be aggressive in whatever they are doing, and do it with all their might as unto the Lord."

There was some apprehension about how he would be received on a championship team. That part was easy. From the superstars, Kareem and "Magic," on down, everyone was supportive. Byron Scott, who'd played against Green in the PAC-10, became an especially good friend.

But Green missed the intense Christian fellowship he had enjoyed in college. After his experience in Hermiston, Rod Bragado encouraged A. C. to get involved in a church. At OSU, he had joined the Maranatha Church on campus. It was a small congregation — only twelve his freshman year — that grew to more than eighty students during his four years there.

Now he could attend Sunday services only rarely because of basketball commitments, but he compensated by participating in mid-week activities at the Maranatha Church on the USC campus. His roommate at his new apartment was a campus evangelist for the church. "I'm not able to go to church all the time," he admitted, "but church starts inside the heart." He also maintained a discipline of prayer and Bible study, and you can't talk with him for long without his faith coming up during the natural course of conversation.

"There's a saying that if Jesus is not Lord over all, then He's not Lord at all," A. C. said, explaining his dedication to Christ. "Jesus wants full participation." He quoted from the Old Testament prophet, Jeremiah: " 'Let not the wise man boast of his wisdom, and let not the mighty man boast of his might, let not a rich man boast of his riches; but let him who boasts boast of this, that he understands and knows Me, that I am the LORD.'

"I don't want to boast about what I can do on the court. I want to know and understand God. That's my goal. I know God is going to use me and I want to make myself available to Him. I'm willing to make that sacrifice."

On the court, the Los Angeles Lakers had made the sacrifice .to be among the best in basketball and A. C.

Green had sacrificed to become an integral part of that team. But listening to him talk, one sensed that the mark A. C. Green will leave on this world will go far beyond any basketball court.

Bobby Jones

4

MR. D
TEAMS WITH DR. J
Bobby Jones

It was New Year's Eve. Celebrants were flocking into the hotel lobby, enjoying complimentary champagne as a prelude to a long night of partying. Bobby Jones and the other members of the Philadelphia 76ers hurried through the jubilant crowd and escaped up the elevators to their rooms.

It had been a long day. After a game the previous night in Sacramento, fog had forced the team to bus

to San Francisco for an alternate flight to Portland.
They'd arrived five hours late and had missed practice.

It would be a long night, too. Three thousand miles
away from their families, they would be holed up in their
rooms, trying to catch some sleep as partiers whooped
it up and ran up and down the stairs and through the
halls.

The team had left home on Christmas Day and
would not return to Philadelphia for another week as
they played six West Coast teams. This was a critical
test for the Sixers who had only recently started playing
like one of the better teams in the league. It was especially important for the famed "Doctor," Julius Erving.
The fifteen-year veteran was trying to decide his future
after this season and he'd hinted that it could hinge on
his and the team's performance during this road trip.

So far the results looked good. The team had struggled earlier in the season and had only a .500 record by
mid-December. Then coach Matt Guokas had juggled
the lineup, moving Julius to guard and starting Bobby
Jones, one of the league's premiere sixth men, at forward
for the first time in several years. The team had lost
one, then reeled off seven straight wins.

"I was unhappy with the way we were starting
games," Guokas had explained. "We weren't coming
out with the intensity I thought we needed defensively.
By putting Bobby in there, you have one of the best defensive players in the league. You know he's going to
get back on defense. Plus I thought it might shake up
the other teams a bit to have to adjust to Julius in the

back court. I don't know how long we're going to stay with this lineup but so far it's worked out well."

Win number seven the previous night had been a strange game. Playing the Kings in the NBA's smallest and noisiest arena, the Sixers had struggled and were down by two points with 1:30 left to play. Bobby Jones hadn't scored a single point. But after a couple of steals and some clutch shooting, he ended up scoring the team's final seven points as Philadelphia squeaked by 87-84. "We didn't deserve to win," Bobby admitted as he relaxed in his room. About his heroics, he was grateful. "When you don't score, you often don't feel a part of the team. I praise the Lord for that one."

Despite his 6.5 points-per-game scoring average, Bobby didn't need to be ashamed of his contributions. True, he didn't fill up the basket like Dr. J or other famous teammates like Charles Barkley and Maurice Cheeks. But Bobby Jones hadn't lasted twelve years in the ABA and NBA because of his scoring.

While Erving had won acclaim as one of the game's greatest offensive stars, Bobby Jones had quietly earned a reputation as one of basketball's top defenders. Eight times he'd been named to the NBA All-Defensive first team. Four times he'd played in the NBA All-Star game. In 1983, he'd won the NBA Sixth Man Award. In 1977 he'd earned the Seagram's Seven Crowns Sports Award as the NBA's "most productive and consistent player."

Bobby had proved that hard work, tough defense, and an attitude that submitted his personal desires to the needs of the team, could lead to a long and profitable career. "He's a dream player," said opposing coach Cotton Fitzsimmons. "He automatically does what you have to beg every other player to do — board, play defense all over, block shots, block out, hustle."

While Bobby's role didn't show up in the box score with spectacular statistics, he enjoyed his reputation. "Actually, Julius can be a much better defensive player than I. Physically he has the talents; it's just a matter of the energy that is demanded in a pro basketball game. You have to sacrifice something. I don't have the offensive ability anyway, so I can get back on defense and maybe pick up his man. Playing defense is mainly effort, and that starts in your mind."

For eight years, Erving's scoring and inspiration and Bobby's defense and sixth man role had helped make Philadelphia an NBA power. But the two stars were not always teammates. In fact, they were on opposing sides for one of the most dramatic confrontations in pro basketball history.

Bobby smiled as he recalled the final ABA championship series in 1976 before the league merged with the NBA. Bobby was an All-Star forward for Denver, the ABA's strongest team. Julius was practically the entire show for the New York Nets. He was the league's most valuable player, and had awed fans with unbelievable moves never seen before on a basketball court. But in a game of five-on-one, Denver figured to win.

As the league's top defensive forward, Bobby was assigned to stop Julius. Years later he shook his head at that audacious thought. "No one could stop him. He handled the ball all the time, and in every game he did something I'd never seen before. He had an uncanny ability to come up with a shot or play to fit the situation."

With four seconds to play in the championship series opener in Denver, Julius had scored 43 points and the game was tied at 118. Naturally the Doctor got the ball, and naturally Bobby guarded him as closely as any human could. Julius launched his shot from the right baseline, eighteen feet from the basket with Bobby's hand in his face. The ball fell cleanly through the net as the buzzer sounded. New York went on to win the title as Dr. J led both teams in every major statistical category.

A few months later, Julius launched the NBA portion of his pro basketball career in Philadelphia, teamed with another individual star, George McGinnis. The team made a run for the NBA title but fell short in the championship series against Portland. Gradually, management realized they had too much offensive firepower — too much individual talent and not enough teamwork — to win the championship. McGinnis was traded to Denver for Jones and the result was a coach's dream.

"The word is *complement,*" explained then-76ers coach Billy Cunningham. "George and Julius tried so hard to complement each other, but I just don't think they were able to do it. I think Bobby will help make us a sounder team. And we'll see the exciting side of Julius Erving." One rival general manager felt Philadelphia had helped themselves at both ends of the court. "Jones will play defense better than anyone else they have, and he'll make Erving that much more effective on offense."

In 1983 Philadelphia finally mustered their talents and defeated Los Angeles for the world championship. Bobby was recognized for his contributions when he was voted the league's Sixth Man Award. Unable to attend the awards ceremony, Bobby asked Julius Erving to accept it on his behalf.

"Bobby epitomizes what is right and good within the NBA," Julius said in the acceptance speech. "He's a tireless worker on the court, always giving his all. He is a model citizen who practices what he preaches. If Bobby were here today, I'm sure he would enjoy accepting this award. But more importantly, he would enjoy the opportunity to give all the honor and glory to Jesus Christ, who guides Bobby through . . . life."

In many ways Bobby and Julius are opposites. Dr. J is flashy on the court, outgoing off it, popular with fans and media, involved in numerous business ventures. Bobby does the gut work on the court while others receive the headlines. He prefers that, being shy and private. Though personable, Bobby is more comfortable away from basketball, with his family, than in public.

However, the two stars discovered a bond that transcended their differences on and off the court. Bobby, who'd given his life to Jesus Christ as a student at North Carolina, started a chapel program with the Sixers during the 1978-79 season. "The first one we had was in Milwaukee. I printed up invitations for both teams and three guys came — Julius, myself, and Kent Benson from the Bucks."

At that time most NBA players were very quiet about their personal faith. Chapels were just starting, but no one was accepting the leadership. Two years later, Julius made a public statement about his faith in Christ at a banquet for the Fellowship of Christian Athletes. Before a stunned crowd of about 1,800 that included Bobby and other area athletes, Julius revealed that he'd asked Christ into his life in July of 1979. "I felt that I would start to understand what my true purpose was for being," he explained. "Since then, I think I have (gained) an understanding of who I am."

"Julius is very much a thinking man," said Bobby, reflecting on the change he's seen in his teammate's life. "He's always been a good guy. But spiritually, I've seen a maturity and growth and a commitment to serve God. He thinks a lot about his role in this life and the effect it can have on other people. I appreciate that about him.

"Another thing I appreciate about Julius is that he's an encourager. One reason I've enjoyed my years in Philadelphia is because of his steadiness. He's quick to say thanks for a nice pass. When we lose, he never points the finger. He's your friend, win or lose. That means a lot."

Bobby's own commitment to Christ had come through the influence of his girlfriend Tess (now his wife) when he was a student at North Carolina. He'd postponed accepting Christ several times because of his commitment to basketball. Then shortly before his senior year, he made his decision after recognizing that matters of eternity were far more important than a basketball career lasting a few years at best. Throughout his pro career, Bobby had been a quiet but powerful spokesman for his faith.

With Julius now committed to Christ, the two teamed up to help spread the faith throughout the league. They sponsored several conference calls linking Christian players. "It was mostly for encouragement," Bobby explained. "It was a chance to share different ideas and to encourage those who were having problems — perhaps the coach didn't like the chapel program — to hang in there.

"The thing the calls and chapel have done is let players know there are other people who care about *them*, not just their basketball. Guys are very skeptical about who to confide in and who to share their problems with. This has been a vehicle for people to open up a bit."

Bobby's faith is reflected in his attitude on the court. He has felt that he should submit his own preferences to the desires of the coach or owner for the good of the team. He is also known as one of the cleanest players in the game; he's never had a technical called against him in the NBA.

"I don't want to paint too rosy a picture," he said. "My first year in the ABA I got thrown out of a game. A guy hit me from behind and knocked me down. I got up and swung at him and they threw us both out. It taught me that fighting is a waste of time. I've prayed since that the Lord would give me control when things get out of hand."

He admitted that, like anyone, he got frustrated at times. He wasn't afraid to get physical under the boards — that's an essential part of the game. "But I've never tried to elbow somebody on purpose." And when someone took a cheap shot at him, Bobby's form of retaliation was "to increase my level of play. I try to beat my man down the court and embarrass him through the score."

He illustrated by telling a story. "I don't want to mention the player's name. But the guy was giving me a lot of elbows and intentional roughness that wasn't necessary. I was frustrated by it and at halftime I prayed that the Lord would guide me through it. As I was praying, this thought came to my mind: 'No weapon that is formed against you shall prosper.' It's a scripture verse from Isaiah but at the time I didn't know where it came from.* The guy fouled out early in the second half and I played well the rest of the game and we ended up coming from behind to win."

Not every episode has such a happy ending, but Bobby's record indicated that his policy paid long-term dividends.

When one watched Bobby Jones on the basketball court, he looked almost frail in comparison to the hefty giants of the game. Sure, he's 6'9", but he's thin and looks like he'd snap in two if bounced by someone like

---

* It's Isaiah 54:17

Daryl Dawkins. It was amazing he'd lasted more than twelve years in the pros.

It was even more incredible when one realized that he'd battled personal health problems. He took medication daily to control epilepsy. For a while he had a problem with an irregular heartbeat, and the medication for that condition didn't mix well with the medication for his epilepsy. Fortunately, the heart problem has disappeared, and concerning his epilepsy, he said, "I gave it to the Lord eight or nine years ago. It's a fact of life and I don't worry about it. I see it as just another opportunity to share my faith."

For all of his success, Bobby Jones isn't in love with basketball. He admitted the game had provided a great life, but he was ready to walk away from it when the time came. Each summer, he left the game behind and concentrated on his family and other interests. He taught at some basketball camps, but only if he was also allowed to talk about his faith.

"My priorities are different from those of a lot of pro basketball players. Their whole life revolves around who they are as a player. For me, who I am is who I am in Jesus Christ. When basketball is through, I will have very little use for it."

It was dark outside now and in a few minutes Bobby would go out for dinner with a representative from Nike shoes. It would be his one brief escape from the confines of the room. Later, he would spend the holiday with his family — by telephone. They were waiting for his call in North Carolina. "My big part of the day is when

I call and talk to them. Unfortunately, the holiday is like any other work day for us.

"Sometimes my kids are a little moody and resentful of the fact I'm not home. Sometimes I get resentful. I wish I could put the children to bed at night. That's one of the things I'm looking forward to most when I leave the game — a more regular schedule."

Twenty-four hours later, the Philadelphia 76ers were hard at work. Fans who had already watched a couple of New Year's Day bowl games came to the basketball game expecting more great action. They weren't disappointed as Portland and Philly played one of the better games of the season. The lead changed hands 22 times and there were 17 ties.

It was a game full of spectacular plays. The Doctor invented another one of his unique moves. On a drive to the hoop in the middle of the second quarter, he rolled the ball from his hand into the crook of his arm to protect it against a defender, then slammed it home.

The game went into overtime before Philly pulled out its eighth straight win, 121-119. Bobby played 32 minutes, made all 4 of his field goal attempts and 2 free throws for 10 points. But once again his real contribution on defense was not measured in the box score. In the final seconds he deflected a pass to deny Portland a good shot at tying the score.

Coach Guokas praised his defense after the game. "We tightened up to make Portland take shots it didn't want to take in its last two possessions." Meanwhile

Bobby dressed quietly while the night's leading scorers had to answer numerous questions from the press.

There was a satisfaction in another job well done, coupled with an anticipation of the future. "I haven't absolutely made the decision to retire after this year," he said. "But right now my wife and I feel I probably won't play. We've bought a house in Charlotte, North Carolina, and we'll be moving down there next summer."

He was looking forward to the opportunity to get involved in several projects. He wanted to do volunteer work for programs like the Fellowship of Christian Athletes and Prison Fellowship. His new home is geared to entertaining: It includes a swimming pool, and Bobby doesn't even enjoy swimming. "We want it to be a place where college groups and church groups can come over and relax," he said. "I want to show people that you don't have to take cocaine or drink beer to have fun."

For now the fun times would have to wait. There was a plane to catch the next morning and another game in Houston in two nights. That meant more time away from the family. But he knew it was temporary. It wouldn't be long before his travels would cease and he could begin to live a normal life. Like enjoying Christmas and New Year's at home.

Steve Colter

Terry Porter

Kiki Vandeweghe

Sam Bowie

Mychal Thompson

5

GIVING GOD HIS DUE

The Portland Trail Blazers

It was an hour until tip-off, but fans were already filing into the perennially sold-out Memorial Coliseum in Portland, Oregon. Some moved immediately to their seats and munched on hot dogs and popcorn. Others ate more substantially in the Coliseum Club. Still others stood under the basket and watched several players from the visiting team practice free throws and jump shots.

Underneath the stands, several members of the home team made their way down the hall to a whitewashed room that served as an extra locker room for such events as the state boys high school basketball tournament. In an adjacent room, a group of girls from a local dance team that would provide half-time entertainment were giggling as they curled their hair and applied their makeup.

Al Egg, a broad-shouldered man whose appearance and athletic background seemed better suited for wrestling than basketball, welcomed the Blazers as they entered the room. Guard Steve Colter, with a smile that made him a favorite among Blazer fans, warmly shook Al's hand. Rookie Terry Porter was more serious as he, too, shook Al's hand.

Veteran center/forward Mychal Thompson, then with the Blazers, went right to the chalkboard and wrote:

Terry Porter: 18 Pts, 10 Assts, 5 Reb, 0 Turnovers

He put the chalk down and commented, "That's what we expect from you tonight!" Then he told Al, "I've got to keep the rookie on his toes."

Al, who does a weekly sports show on a local Christian radio station, never knew quite what to expect from Mychal, the team's resident humorist. Once during a fifteen-minute interview Mychal called Al "the Howard Cosell of the gospel," tabbed himself as golf's "Black Nicklaus," and aspired to be a color commentator after pro ball, saying, "I'm already colored, so I'm halfway there."

Center Sam Bowie dipped his head as he came through the door. He shook Al's hand, sat down and pulled off one of his size-seventeen sneakers. Sam had problems with a sore big toe and he pulled out the insole of the shoe in order to try to make his foot more comfortable. The last person to enter was forward Kiki Vandeweghe. He slipped in almost unnoticed, nodded to Al, and sat upright on one of the benches.

It was time for chapel, a voluntary meeting that is part of the pre-game routine for every Blazer home game. Often, members of the visiting team join the Blazers for the fifteen-minute devotional period when players can meditate, pray, and contemplate the spiritual dimension of life.

The chaplain is Al Egg, a former businessman turned ordained minister who admits with embarrassment that his pre-Christian days were filled with carousing. After a dramatic conversion, Al gave up his business in order to devote himself to a full-time ministry with Portland area high school, college, and pro teams.

Veteran center/forward Mychal Thompson is one of the reasons chapel is an established part of the Blazers program. Along with former Blazer Kelvin Ransey, he asked coach Jack Ramsey for permission to hold the meeting before the team took the court for warmups.

Ramsey, who has since moved on to coach the Indiana Pacers, was supportive. "An awareness of a supreme being is important for everybody's emotional and spiritual well-being," Ramsey explained. "I think in most instances it enhances preparation. It keeps a player's emotional level at a proper point." Mychal's reason for initiating the services was more personal: "I needed a time to give God His due."

This evening's meeting started with a prayer by Mychal. It was simple and direct: "Heavenly Father, we thank You for this opportunity to get together tonight. Guide Al now and give him words of wisdom. Carry us through this game and let us be shining examples of You on the floor tonight. In Christ's name we pray, Amen."

The Blazers chaplain doesn't really preach; his style is more of a dialogue in which he helps players gain insights from the Bible. Al started this evening by asking the players to think about the famine in Ethiopia. "When you see pictures of starving children in Africa, doesn't that make you feel grateful for all you have?"

Steve Colter nodded enthusiastically. Sam Bowie continued to work on his shoe while he listened. The others stared intently at the speaker.

"Or when you drive down Burnside Street here in Portland and see the drunks who spend the night on the curb; aren't you grateful that you have a home and the opportunity to live the way you do? And when you see pictures of India, doesn't that make you grateful that God has blessed this country the way He has?

"I'd like for you to think a minute of all the kids who were your teammates in high school. How many of them went on to play college ball? And how many of your college teammates went on to play pro ball? Kiki, can you think of someone in high school who had more talent than you?"

Kiki gave a slight nod.

"I'm sure all of you can think of someone who had more talent, but wasted it. You men were given a certain amount of talent, and you worked hard to maximize it and become what you are today."

Al opened his Bible to the Gospel of Luke. "In chapter 17 we read the story of Jesus healing ten lepers." Al briefly summarized the story: The lepers stood at a distance and shouted, "Jesus, have mercy on us!" Jesus told them to go and show themselves to the priests. As they started toward the temple, they were all healed. But only one of the ten returned to thank Jesus and praise God for the miracle.

To help the players understand the significance of this story, Al explained that leprosy was a dreaded skin disease. Those who had it were outcasts from society. If they came within a hundred feet of anyone who was not a leper, they had to yell, "Unclean! Unclean!" as a warning. Al asked the players if they could think of any similar disease today.

Sam Bowie, finished tying his shoe, suggested, "Wouldn't it be like having AIDS?"

"To a certain extent, yes," Al answered. "Certainly both are devastating. But if anyone of you in this room had AIDS right now, the rest of us wouldn't know unless you told us. But if anyone had leprosy, we'd all know it."

The lesson from this story was simple: "Do you think you'd be grateful if God healed you of something that bad?"

"You bet!" exuded Colter, and the other players agreed.

"I'm convinced that these ten lepers couldn't help but be grateful. One moment they had no contact with society. The next they were totally healed and were allowed to resume a normal life. All of them had to be grateful. But notice, only one of them took the time to come back to Jesus and *thank* Him. All were grateful, but only one was thankful.

"Tonight, I'd like for us to take a moment to thank God for some of the things for which we're grateful. What are some of the things we can thank God for?"

"Our families," said Colter.

"The chance to play pro ball," said Terry.

"For good health," said Mychal.

Al acknowledged the answers and then invited Steve Colter to close the meeting in prayer. "Lord, we do have so much to be thankful for," Steve prayed. "We thank you for our families, and for healthy bodies that allow us to play in the greatest pro league in the world. And thank you for Al who has ministered to us. Now, Lord, please protect us tonight from any injury, and help us give our best for Your glory. In Jesus' name we pray, Amen."

As the players filed out of the room, each one warmly thanked Al for the message. It had been a welcome interlude from the hectic pace of their lives. All members of the Blazers are welcome to attend chapel, and several others have participated on occasion. The five regular participants had different reasons for going. "We didn't go to church every Sunday," said Terry Porter about his family. "But I find the chapels very helpful, especially during the rough times."

Some of the rough times included an intense competition for playing time at the point guard position with Steve Colter and another Christian teammate, Darnell Valentine. Before Valentine was traded to the Los Angeles Clippers, Colter believed that their faith had provided perspective in a difficult situation.

"We had a chance to understand what the other was going through, instead of being negative toward each other," said Steve. "We were lifting each other up. When I was a rookie, Darnell helped me out, and I've tried to help Terry this year. We all give our hardest and let the coaches make the decisions."

Sam Bowie, who had suffered from leg injuries throughout his college and pro career, attended chapel as a reminder of why he was in the NBA. "The Lord will always be number one in my life," said Sam. "I'm in the position I am because the good Lord put me here. He didn't have to choose me to be in the NBA. There are thousands of other kids who play every day who'd like to be here. So I'm very thankful for this opportunity."

Mychal Thompson was also thankful for the opportunity, but admitted that when he first joined the Blazers as the NBA's top draft choice in 1978, he wasn't a practicing Christian. "I grew up in a Christian home and accepted Jesus Christ as my personal Savior at the age of eleven," he explained. "But I was not living for the Lord. I was running around with the wrong crowd, partying, chasing girls. I was never into drugs, but my priorities were definitely all screwed up."

It took several serious problems — including a leg injury that sidelined him for an entire season, a broken marriage, and a bad financial investment that cost him more than $400,000 — to wake him up. "God spanked me pretty good," he said. "I came back to the Lord in 1984, and I came back to stay."

Kiki Vandeweghe didn't have to endure such traumatic trials to see the light. Though he grew up in a talented family (his mother was Miss America, his father a former NBA player and now a doctor, and his sister swam for the United States in the 1976 Olympics) he did not have exceptional athletic ability. His trail to the NBA required endless hours of practice, often going more than two months without a day off.

"I feel a lot of players are more talented than I am," said Kiki, "and I got a late start playing basketball. So I had to put in a lot of extra work. I couldn't be pleased with myself if I weren't good at what I do."

Kiki's professional basketball career began in a hotbed of controversy. He was drafted by Dallas, but refused to sign. Dallas traded him to Denver. After a sluggish first season, his scoring average exploded, reaching a high of 29.4 during the 1983-84 season. He also started attending chapels at the invitation of teammate Alex English. "It provided fellowship. I really missed going to church, and this provided an avenue for me to discuss things about life and the Lord."

Vandeweghe was the center of another controversy when he was traded to Portland for three players plus first and second round draft choices prior to the 1984-85 season. Many Blazers fans felt their team had surrendered far too much for the scorer. Kiki accepted the problem the way he does all obstacles: "as a way to improve myself. I think the Lord played a big part in my getting over this hump. If I'd just been cast adrift by myself, I would have had great difficulty because there was constant criticism."

Kiki is a regular participant in the Blazers chapels, and appreciates Al Egg's availability. "Most of the time someone wants something from you. It's hard to find people outside your family who will talk to you just for you, not for what you've done.

"Prayer is an important part of my daily life. Any time I have a problem or a major decision, I always consult the Lord. My problems sometimes seem big to me, but He can solve my problems . . . if I just stop and listen."

Steve Colter was one of the most popular Blazers players, not only for his charismatic personality on and off the court, but also for his efforts to serve the community. He pointed to two factors that motivated this involvement. First, as a youngster, he had contact with several members of the Phoenix Suns who often visited the Boys Club in Phoenix, Arizona. Connie Hawkins, in particular, impressed on Steve and the other boys the importance of doing well in studies at school.

The other influence was his commitment to Christ during his junior year at Phoenix Union High School. With 12,000 students in the school, there was plenty of opportunity for him to go astray. But he saw the tragic results of the kids who chose drugs, crime and good times over school and athletics. He decided to instead follow Jesus Christ and reach out to those who weren't as fortunate. "I think God definitely led me in the right way."

In Portland, Steve organized a motivational program for students in cooperation with the Avia shoe company. "First we'd bring to practice a classroom of kids who weren't getting their homework done. I'd shoot some baskets and talk with them about the importance of a good education."

That was enough to motivate some kids to dramatically improve their school work. So Steve, along with Avia and the Blazers, further developed a program that provided tickets to sold-out Blazers games as an incentive for improved grades and increased reading performance.

Steve's life-long dream is "to tell more people about Jesus Christ." After his career in pro basketball is over, he wants to put his faith and experience to good use. "I plan to get my degree in clinical psychology and I would like to work with the mentally retarded and mentally handicapped. I feel that's what Christ wants me to do."

Chaplain Al Egg is often amazed at the variety of players who attend the chapel services and are looking for spiritual direction. "All I do is tell them about Jesus," he said after one service. "The chapel program is available because the players requested it. A number of players have indicated that it provides balance to their lives and helps them deal with the pressures that are unique to NBA life."

For a moment, Al reflected on his unusual position. "I'm here because the players asked me. As long as they want me, I'll continue to do it."

Photo courtesy of Utah Jazz

Mark Eaton

6

THE MOUNTAIN MAN

Mark Eaton

Many pro basketball experts thought Utah had wasted a draft pick on Mark Eaton in 1982. Three years later he was named the league's Defensive Player of the Year. For years, the Jazz were the joke of the league. Now, the laugh is Utah's, a team that won its first division title and made its first playoff appearances — with Mark Eaton at center.

Reporters have nicknamed him Mountain Man, the Eclipse, the Great Wall of China, Skyscraper, the Rock of Gibraltar, and King Kong. Former Portland coach Jack Ramsey doesn't use any nicknames, but the 7'4", 295-pound giant has given Ramsey a few headaches. Against Ramsey's Blazers one season, Mark blocked 47 shots in five games. "When a guy blocks 10 shots in a game, he's taking away 10 potential scores," says Ramsey. "Each block can cause a 4-point turnaround. To beat him, we have to adjust with more movement, using the fast break and better shot selection."

The Blazers aren't the only NBA team to find the going tough against the Jazz center. During the 1984-85 season, Eaton set a league record for blocked shots with 456, twice as many as runnerup Akeem Olajuwon of Houston, and more than thirteen entire teams. Chicago coach Stan Albeck says, "You can't shoot anything in 'the paint' over the guy." Mark also wound up fifth in the league in rebounds, and first in defensive boards. Says former Philadelphia coach Billy Cunningham, "He's never going to be a player who's pretty. He's just going to win games for you."

Mark Eaton's story is an incredible, Bunyanesque tale about how an oversized teenager overcame schoolboy taunts to become a standout professional center. *After* a three-year detour as an auto mechanic, and a non-career at the UCLA basketball factory.

In the land of NBA giants, Mark Eaton is the biggest. He's not as tall as Washington's 7'7" Ugandan import, Manute Bol, or the 7'5" twelfth man for Detroit, Chuck

Nevitt. But his combination of bulk and height actually make centers like Boston's Robert Parish look small. That's the only reason Utah even drafted him. "You can't coach height," quipped Jazz coach and general manager Frank Layden.

Everywhere he goes, Mark must endure gawks and stares from the curious. Today, Mark is comfortable with that fact of life, but there was a time when he wanted to run from the inevitable questions:

"How tall are you?"

"How's the weather up there?"

"What basketball team do you play for?"

For several years, Mark didn't play for any basketball team. "I didn't have a very positive experience with athletics in high school," he explains. "I felt it was unfair that people should automatically assume I was a basketball player just because I was tall."

It wasn't that Mark didn't like sports. It's just that his primary interest was water polo. Needless to say, he was a formidable goalie. But during his senior year in high school, he yielded to pressure and joined the basketball team. Trouble was, no one knew how to coach him, so he sat at the end of the bench and endured the taunts of insensitive students. No college basketball factories, or even little sweatshops, came calling for his services. Mark was so disgusted with the sport that he decided to attend an Arizona trade school after graduation, where he learned to be an auto mechanic.

It was a natural choice. Mark's 6'9" father was a diesel mechanic, so he had spent a lot of time around engines. "I knew I wasn't going to do it my whole life," he says. "But it was something I could make a good living at."

Mark was twenty-one years old, three years out of high school, when Tom Lubin happened by the Mark C. Bloom Tire Store where Mark was working in Buena Park, California. Tom was a chemistry professor and the basketball coach at Cypress Junior College just down the street. Tom took one look at the mechanic and made his first recruiting pitch. Mark told him to "get lost."

Fortunately for Mark and the basketball world, Tom was persistent. Lubin understood tall men. His uncle had played center for the 1932 Olympic team and taught Tom many secrets of the pivot. Tom had discovered 6'11" Swen Nater and tutored him using the uncle's expertise. Swen, who never played high school basketball, had gone on to a pro career after two years backing up Bill Walton at UCLA.

For two months, Tom was a regular visitor at the tire store. He had Swen Nater drop by for a chat. He left literature that Mark tossed unread into a drawer. Finally, Tom issued a challenge: "Just work out with me for two hours next Sunday. I want to show you a few basic moves because I think you'll be amazed how simple this game is." Hoping that would end the harassment, Mark accepted.

The session on an asphalt court was a surprise to
Mark. "Tom showed me some moves designed specifically for centers — a little step across the key and hook
shot; a little turn, drop step, bounce the ball once and
take a shot; a turnaround bank shot. For the first time,
I felt I had some coordination." It was enough to convince Mark to give the sport a try, but not enough to
quit his job and attend school full time. Mark enrolled
at Cypress, but worked every morning, went to practice
in the afternoon, and took classes at night. "I figured
if basketball didn't work out, I'd still have my job."

Under Tom's tutelage, the twenty-two-year-old freshman averaged nearly 14 points and 11 rebounds as the
team won 34 of 36 games. After the season, he was
drafted by the Phoenix Suns in the fifth round. Mark
knew he wasn't ready to turn pro, but it motivated him
to see how far he could go. "Tom and I felt I'd get
more training if I stayed in college," says Mark. "Plus,
if I did go pro and it didn't work out, then what would
I do? That was when I decided to try to make a career
out of basketball."

So Mark quit his mechanic's job and worked part
time selling cars and as a bouncer at a disco. During
his sophomore season at Cypress, he helped the team
win the state junior college title. Now the big-college
coaches were drooling at the prospect of having Mark
in their program. All except UCLA. The ten-time national
champions wouldn't turn him away, but they had plenty
of high school all-Americans who wanted to play there,
too. Mark chose the Bruins primarily because he couldn't
resist the challenge.

The next two years were perhaps the most trying of
Mark's life. To help people understand how he survived,
he relates an experience that occurred while he was in
high school: "Our family went to a Lutheran church
while I was growing up. When I was sixteen, I went to a
retreat with the church youth group and there the leader
started talking to me about how God loved me and had
a plan for my life. Until then, I'd never realized that I
needed to have a personal relationship with Christ.
From that point forward I became a much more avid
Christian."

Mark's faith in Jesus Christ is quiet but steady. He
doesn't talk a lot about it, but it's there and it's real. At
UCLA, he needed that foundation. The Bruins were
coming off a second-place finish in the NCAA finals.
They were a small, quick team and Coach Larry Brown
used Mark for only 155 minutes over the entire season.
"That was difficult to deal with mentally," he admits.
"I kept in close touch with Tom and he told me I'd
have to do what Swen did and make the practices my
games."

So Mark made every workout count and put in
many more hours of solo work. And he prayed. "I
asked God, 'Is this what You planned for me?' I couldn't
see coming this far and God just saying, 'Now forget
it, let's do something else.' I felt He had some sort of
plan, and I had to stick with it and follow it through."

That summer Larry Farmer replaced Brown as head
coach. When Mark asked what he could do to improve,

Coach Farmer typed out a list of basketball and conditioning drills. Mark devoted the rest of the summer to rigorous training in the morning and pick-up games, often against NBA players, in the afternoon.

The new Mark Eaton impressed Farmer and his assistants. They indicated he might even have a shot at the starting center position. But when the season opened, a freshman had the job. No one explained why. Mark just sat. And waited. He played a grand total of 41 minutes that year, the equivalent of one game. The final insult came as the team was preparing for its last road trip of the season: Mark was told to stay home.

Even for a normally calm and gentle man, that was too much. Two trash cans went flying across the gym, and he admits that it was a good thing the coaches weren't there at the moment, "because I don't know if I could have been responsible for my actions."

After he cooled down, there was more prayer. And Tom had an idea. The pair traveled to San Diego to see old friend Swen Nater, now in his ninth pro season. Nater introduced them to the assistant coach of the Clippers, who recommended a couple of basketball camps where perhaps a pro scout or two might see him play. Mark paid his way to Cincinnati and Jersey City to participate in those camps. But it looked like Mark's best chance was to play pro ball in Europe for a year or two, then hope for a chance at the big time.

Enter the Jazz, a team that had never managed a winning record since their birth in 1974. They were 20th (out of 23 teams) in blocked shots, 22nd in points allowed, and last in rebounding. Their occasional wins came on nights when their offense was hot enough to outscore the opposition. General manager Frank Layden requested a highlight tape of Mark from UCLA, then complained that all he saw was "a few pictures of him taking off his warmups." Nevertheless, the Jazz selected Mark in the fourth round.

Fourth-round draft choices are not a hot commodity in the NBA. In fact, after the first round, most draft choices find themselves fortunate to play the exhibition season before getting cut. Occasionally, a team keeps a player as a "project" with hopes for a return on their investment after a year or two. Successful projects in the NBA are about as common as clear photographs of Bigfoot.

"Mark didn't come into this league with a lot of God-given talents," Coach Layden admits. "Most players were all-Americans in high school and college and everyone's paid them all sorts of homage. Mark never had that and he came in hungry, with that little-boy attitude. And he beat all the odds."

To relieve some of the immediate pressure on Mark, Layden offered to guarantee the first year of Mark's contract. That bought some time to learn the pro game. Under the tutelage of assistant coach Phil Johnson, Eaton worked diligently during the off-season on weight training, conditioning and technique. "He was willing to work when he was alone," says Layden, with the admiration of a proud father. "It's easy to go out and play in summer leagues with your teammates. But it's not a lot of fun to go out and drill and exercise and lift weights and run. He's dedicated himself to doing the work and it's paid off."

Mark, by his own admission, was "a little rough around the edges." But in the second game of his first season, he managed seven blocked shots against Dallas as the Jazz won. What Mark discovered was that he could affect the outcome of games just by raising his forty-one-inch arms. Flat-footed, he came within six inches of the rim. Players would drive the lane and throw a fancy move or two, but the mountain wouldn't budge. Though he could jump only eight to ten inches, that was often enough to alter a shot, or deflect the ball to a teammate, sparking a Jazz fast break.

With more playing time, Mark's confidence increased. Then in mid-season, the Jazz traded center Danny Schayes to Denver and Mark replaced him in the starting lineup. He finished third in the league in blocked shots. And though Utah still lost more games than they won, they were losing by closer scores. It was obvious that this team was significantly closer to being a winner, especially because 30-points-per-game scorer Adrian Dantley, who'd missed most of the season, was regaining his health.

Mark continued to work hard in the off-season, reducing his body fat from eighteen percent — average for an auto mechanic but too soft for an NBA player — to eleven percent. In the 1983-84 season, Utah shocked the pro basketball world by posting its first winning season ever and capturing the Midwest Division title in the process. Mark led the league in blocked shots, averaging more than four per game. In their first playoff appearance, Utah defeated Denver in the first round before losing to Phoenix in six rugged games.

When Mark talks about his dramatic rise to respect within the NBA, he also reveals how his faith has motivated him to give his very best effort. "I don't think Christians should be wimps," he says. "God doesn't want to see some guy go out on the basketball court and get pushed around and knocked down and beaten all the time. What kind of an example is that?

"I determined that every minute I was out on the court, I was going to give 110 percent so people would say, 'Mark Eaton may not have the most talent in the world, but he's out there night in and night out busting his rear end.' God has taken care of me, but I've also worked very hard."

Mark got a clearer picture of just how God was taking care of him when in the first round of the 1985 playoffs he injured his knee against Houston. He'd battled hard through four games against the twin towers of Akeem Olajuwon and Ralph Sampson. Then in the second quarter of the deciding contest, a player accidentally rolled into his knee at the end of a play. The preliminary observation on the bench was not encouraging. On the flight home, Mark and his wife, Marcie, faced an uncertain future.

"All sorts of things go through your mind," he says. "I was just coming off my best season. We had been talking about renegotiating my contract, then suddenly I'm facing what may be a career-ending injury. Right then, I said to God, 'Whatever You want me to do now is fine. If You want me to stop playing basketball, I'll go home and get out my tool box and go back to work as a mechanic.' I no longer had a fear of failure. I knew God was controlling my life and I was going to roll with the flow. There was no sense worrying about it."

The injury was not as serious as first feared, but it did require surgery. After a summer of rehabilitation, Mark was back in the lineup for Utah, and his coach was saying that Mark Eaton could become one of the top two or three centers in the league. "He's never going to be a Kareem Abdul-Jabbar," says Layden. "Maybe he'll never be a Pat Ewing. But he's going to be a force in this league."

Mark, for his part, wants to keep improving. "My goal now is to be consistent. Plus, there are a hundred little technical things I can work on. People don't realize that once you're in the NBA, you have to keep working. Adrian Dantley has been in the league eleven years and he's such a great scorer because he continually works on his game."

Mark often reflects on how far he's come and is encouraged. "My life could have gone either way," he says. "I put my faith in God and have developed a relationship with Him where I can totally trust Him."

As a result, Mark is no longer self-conscious about his size. In fact, he's proud to be known as a pro basketball player, and he's glad to let people know who's responsible.

Marques Johnson

7

FINDING
THE RIGHT CRUTCH
Marques Johnson

There were rumors — Marques Johnson is on drugs. For a few days, it provided fodder for gossip columns during the off-season. But the issue died when the small forward for the Milwaukee Bucks overcame a poor season and qualified again for the All-Star game.

Nearly three years later, after a momentous six-player trade between Milwaukee and the Los Angeles Clippers, the rumors resurfaced in *The Los Angeles Times*. Across five columns on the front page of the sports section, the bold headline read: "Questions Arise in Marques Johnson Trade." The subhead explained: "Clippers Say They Didn't Know About His Treatment in a Rehab Center in 1983."

It's unfortunate that one cannot follow professional sports and avoid the issue of drugs. In recent years, drug scandals have riddled professional football, baseball, and basketball. NBA commissioner David Stern found it the one flaw in an otherwise healthy game. In 1986, All-Star guard Micheal Ray Richardson was banned from the league for cocaine use after repeated warnings and extensive attempts at rehabilitation. Then Len Bias, the second pick of the 1986 NBA draft, died suddenly from a heart attack induced by what was apparently his first use of cocaine. These were only the two most visible signs of this sinister problem.

The NBA has tried to develop a realistic plan to address the drug problem. It allows players to come forward in private and receive help. According to the commissioner, "The goal is total rehabilitation. We take the compassionate view. It takes courage on the part of somebody who has a problem to come forward and admit it."

Marques Johnson asked for help and found it. His problem was addressed away from the glare of the press and did not become public knowledge until nearly three years later, when it made headlines in the *Times*. Johnson's coach, Don Chaney, was furious about the publicity. "Things such as this should be forgotten," he said. "If a guy's made a mistake, but he's trying to live a straight life, to have it dragged through the dirt is an injustice. Marques is a changed man."

Unfortunately, the news media could not ignore the fact that at the time of the story, Johnson was suffering through his poorest season in eight years. The article implied that his performance might be drug-related. In fact, Marques had suffered a broken finger on his shooting hand, plus a pulled hamstring and sprained ankle. The broken finger was the primary reason his shooting percentage dropped dramatically and his 16.4 points-per-game scoring average was the lowest of his career. Still, Johnson refused to defend himself when asked to comment about the article.

Others in the Clippers organization weren't afraid to speak up. General manager Carl Scheer, who said he was satisfied at the time of the trade that Marques was not on drugs, was quoted in the *Santa Anna Register* as saying, "I feel so much support for Marques that I'm ready to stand behind and next to him on anything."

Clippers guard Norm Nixon said he couldn't believe the rumors. "I'm no expert on drugs, but I've never seen anything in Marques to indicate a thing."

Harvey Catchings, Marques' teammate both in Milwaukee and Los Angeles, added, "I got mad when I saw the story. I had no idea whatsoever whether Marques was using drugs. I saw no signs when I was in Milwaukee or since we've been with the Clippers."

In fact, the story was true. Marques Johnson had participated in the St. Mary's Drug Rehabilitation Center in Minneapolis for six weeks during the summer of 1982. But it wasn't until the fall of 1985 that he was willing to talk about it. "I wanted to save my family from any embarrassment," he explained when we met one afternoon for a pre-game dinner. "I didn't want them to have to go through the negative stuff that follows such a revelation."

Marques changed his mind after reading some letters to the editor in Los Angeles papers. Several mothers were grateful that an athlete was willing to speak frankly about his problems because it helped their kids. "I realized that kids look up to me and think I'm some god. But I'm human and prone to human mistakes. Reading those letters made me feel that it would be better to let people know what happened, from my point of view, and clear the air on the whole subject."

Marques Johnson is not a drug user now. That doesn't mean he's never tempted, but since he completed his rehabilitation program in 1982, he has experienced victory from the pull of cocaine. Marques emphasizes that his victory is not due to his own efforts, but to a higher power. About that spiritual power he is eager to talk.

As Marques tells his story, it is frightening to realize just how easily someone can be trapped in drugs. He was born in Nachitoches, Louisiana, one of five children. When he was five years old, the family moved to Los Angeles where his parents taught school. In high school, he was already excelling as an athlete. Apart from an occasional puff of marijuana, his life revolved around sports.

His college basketball career at UCLA was sensational. The Bruins won the NCAA championship in 1975, and two years later, Marques was named Collegiate Player of the Year. Milwaukee made him its number one draft choice in 1977, and he was the third player selected in that year's NBA draft. He immediately became the Bucks' second-leading scorer with a 19.5 average and made the All-Rookie team. One year later, his average had escalated to 25.6, third best in the league and good enough for first team NBA All-Star honors.

Despite his obvious success on the floor, Marques was having problems. "I had more money than I knew what to do with, and too much time on my hands. That's a bad combination. I was living by myself in Milwaukee. I didn't really know anyone in the city; it wasn't like L.A. where I had friends and there was lots to do. So I started hanging out at the clubs and discos, trying to meet people. It seemed the natural thing to do — go out after a game, have something to drink, mingle and try to develop a core group of friends."

That seemed innocent enough. Except that drugs, particularly cocaine, was an element of this socializing, though not a significant one during the season. Off-season, however, was party time. Then he could unwind and get high. Once a new season rolled around, he dropped it. For a while, he seemed in total control.

Marques Johnson's first contract with the Bucks expired after the 1980-81 season. Negotiations for a new contract were bitter and the two sides remained far apart when the season opened. As the season headed into December, Marques was still a holdout, and it appeared that he might miss the entire year. That's when his drug problem became serious.

"Up to then, my use of cocaine had been recreational, confined primarily to summertime," he explained. "Now September and October came around I was still at home. November, December, when I'm used to playing basketball, I'm sitting around. My way of placating myself, to cover it up inside, was to medicate the pressure away."

Marques explained the effect cocaine had on him. "The first few times, it seemed great. I felt like I had all the power in the world. Confidence. I could converse with anybody without any reservations, and normally I'm pretty laid back. I was up, energetic. But as it turned out, the more I relied on it, the more of an opposite effect it had. It caused me to think about things too much. At first it helped me put things out of my mind; now it would magnify a lot of those negative thoughts I was trying to hide. As a result, I became more withdrawn. The good feelings were gone and negative feelings were cropping up."

When he no longer appreciated cocaine's effect, it was too late. He discovered he could no longer take it or leave it. "That's when the preoccupation started to set in. I'd wake up in the morning and plan out my day.

'I'm going to work out, do this, take care of some business. Then this evening, I'm going to find some coke and get high.' I found myself looking forward to that time in the evening when I could indulge. That's when I became concerned.

"I don't think too many people knew. My parents probably did. During the off-season I lived with them in L.A. while I was looking for a house. I would come in at all hours of the night and sleep all day. They asked me a couple of times what was going on, and if I was involved in drugs. I denied that anything was wrong."

Marques and the Bucks finally agreed on a contract after twenty-two regular season games. As he resumed play, Marques cut back on the cocaine usage, but his performance on the court fell short of past standards. "I'd never had urges to do coke during basketball season. But now it was like I had to find something to remove the depression. I was playing terribly, the fans were booing and calling me overpaid. In order to hide from those negative things, I'd medicate myself to a point where it didn't matter."

The problem might have continued had not the FBI launched an investigation into cocaine use in Milwaukee. Marques wasn't a target, but his name did surface along with the names of several other pro athletes. Marques learned about the rumors on the radio while driving to a post-season meeting with Bucks' management. His first impulse was to run. Then he realized that maybe this was his chance to get some help.

The coach, general manager, and vice-president of the Bucks met Marques when he arrived at the office. They asked him about the rumors, and Marques said he wasn't selling drugs or using drugs. "They asked me if I had a problem and I told them I didn't think so. They asked me if, rather than my making a rash judgment, I was willing to let professionals determine that. I had a lot of respect for Coach Nelson and Milwaukee had been really generous with me. So I said yes. The whole thing (the rumors) turned out to be a blessing in disguise."

Marques flew to Minnesota to meet with former pro football player Carl Eller, who'd had a drug problem himself while he was a player. With Eller's encouragement, he entered St. Mary's. As he started receiving his education in drugs, Marques recognized many of the danger signals. He was preoccupied with drugs. He was trying to hide it from others. He was rationalizing the danger.

"It wasn't a conscious rationalization," he explained. "I knew there was always the chance I could get stopped and searched, but I would always think about that after the fact. Then I'd think I was lucky, and it would never happen to me."

The process of rehabilitation surprised him. Marques Johnson learned that he could not solve the problem on his own. He needed a higher source. For that, he looked to his spiritual roots. On his mother's side of the family were several Baptist ministers. As a child, church and Sunday school were an important part of the family's weekly activities. Marques had stopped going only when he reached high school and was allowed to choose for himself.

Rejection of his spiritual heritage brought confusion in college. "There were so many philosophies on campus. Islam. TM. All kinds of things were thrown at me. Though I had a strong Christian background, I wanted to search for something else. Before my sophomore year I worked extremely hard to get ready for the basketball season. Three days before practice started, I came down with hepatitis. For a while, doctors wondered if I'd play at all that year. I lost about twenty pounds in one week.

"My teammate, Ralph Drollinger (a 7'2" center), visited my room. He'd always been an avid Bible reader and I respected him. We held hands and prayed and I verbally accepted the Lord Jesus Christ into my heart. That was the first time I could remember doing that."

Marques returned to health much faster than expected. Once he was back playing basketball, the impact of his prayer diminished. Occasionally, when he had a problem he'd pray, and Ralph gave him some literature to read. But there was no church involvement, no Bible study, and no one to talk to, especially after Ralph graduated that spring. His roommate the next year was a Moslem. Marques described that period of his life like this: "It was like a seed that is planted, but the vine gets choked by the thorns before it can really grow and mature."

Seven years later at St. Mary's, Marques Johnson was told to center his thoughts on a source higher than himself. "We had to stop focusing on ourselves. We had to realize that in trying to do things through our own power, we were going to screw up. Through prayer and meditation, we had to ask for strength and guidance. So I began to pray for strength, realizing that I could only be delivered from cocaine in the name of Jesus. I was no longer in the driver's seat. I had to submit to Jesus Christ."

Marques Johnson was a different man after he completed the treatment. But the battle wasn't over. It was one thing to be educated in a rehabilitation center; it was another to prove the change was real among the everyday pressures and temptations of professional basketball. He knew he could not survive alone.

He solicited the help of a brother-in-law who is a professional counselor. The two talked often and Marques was frequently reminded that he had spiritual power, through Christ, that he could claim over his enemy. He also joined a church in Milwaukee.

Before the 1982-83 season, Junior Bridgeman approached Marques about participating in a Bible study along with teammates Harvey Catchings and Lorenzo Romar. "We wanted to relate how we dealt with adversity and pressure," says Bridgeman, who also came to the Clippers in the Johnson-Cummings swap. "I had tried to deal with them myself, and that only made me feel worse. I learned that the limelight isn't going to last. Only one thing will last, and that's a relationship with

God. So we started having Bible studies and found peace of mind. We started in the Gospels, learning about Jesus and what His life means to us today. In the process, Marques discovered that he was able to deal with things that had bothered him in the past."

Two things particularly helped with the temptation to do coke. First, Marques remembered a verse in the Bible: " 'Therefore if any man be in Christ, he is a new creation; old things are passed away; behold, all things are become new.'* I kept remembering that the old me did those things. Now I had a new me that could reap all the benefits of a relationship with Jesus Christ."

He also remembered that the old Marques Johnson wasn't a very likable person. He cringes when he thinks about what he was like under the influence of drugs, especially how he treated the people he loved. "I became so preoccupied with being high that I neglected my responsibilities. Small things like acknowledging birthdays. Or the family would gather for a celebration and I'd think, 'I'll get a little high, then go.' Then I'd feel paranoid that I was too high, so I'd skip it altogether. The next day I'd feel guilty. Those memories are a strong deterrent."

The new Marques Johnson regained his old basketball skills. His scoring average returned to 20-plus points per game, and he appeared in the 1983 All-Star game. But while drugs were a thing of the past, his problems were not over. Marques had never felt at home in Milwaukee and desired to return to his hometown and play before his friends and family. A close Christian friend in Los Angeles, Ed Waters, had prayed with him about a trade to L.A. That prayer was answered just prior to the 1984-85 season. The move turned out to be a nightmare. The injuries and resulting drop in production, followed by the revelations in *The Los Angeles Times,* led to an important discovery.

"I made my request to God about the trade, and God answered. But He also had some expectations of me and that's where I fell short. I didn't follow up on my commitment as strongly as I should have. I neglected my Bible reading and stopped going to church. That's why the adversity didn't affect me the way it could have. I realized that I had some owning up to do. It wasn't that God was treating me bad. He was showing me that I needed to move to the next level of commitment.

"Romans 12:2 tells us to not be conformed to this world, but to be transformed by the renewing of our minds. The reason is so we can show what is the good, and perfect, and acceptable will of God. For me, I'd been doing the good for some time. Now God wanted me to move on to the perfect and acceptable. I needed to make even more of a commitment. I'm learning to meditate on things that are true and good and pure. I'm listening mostly to Christian music. I'm trying to let God build me from the inside out. I know I'll never reach the point where I'm perfect, but that's what I strive for."

Coach Don Chaney was pleased with the results during the 1985-86 season when Marques regained his All-Star level of performance. "If I could pick someone to be my son, Marques would be the guy," said Chaney after Johnson was selected to play in the 1986 All-Star game. "I love what he represents. He has great integrity and character. He's kept this team together . . . he was a stabilizing force during the period where we were losing games."

Marques Johnson has learned some important lessons during his pro basketball career. About his experience with drugs, he says, "It didn't take long for me to realize I had grabbed the wrong crutch. I made a terrible mistake, and I'm still paying for it."

But with this mistake, hope has emerged. "There comes a point in our lives where we start looking for crutches, for things to lean on. I would say, lean on Jesus. Everything else is going to pass away. But when you lean on Jesus, He will strengthen you and help you."

---

* 2 Corinthians 5:17 (New Scofield Reference Edition)

Butch Carter

8

SKIPPING
THE EASY WAY OUT
Butch Carter

A horde of radio, television, and newspaper reporters invaded the steamy visitors' locker room. A half-dressed Patrick Ewing looked down at the herd and prepared to endure another round of questions. The man known as the next Bill Russell, Wilt Chamberlain, or Kareem Abdul-Jabbar — depending on the reporter's preference — was making his first tour of the western states as a member of the New York Knicks. A large media contingent was reporting every move he made and every word he uttered.

In the hall outside the room, another crowd of reporters pestered beleaguered Knicks coach Hubie Brown. His team might have won the best center to emerge from the college ranks in several years, but Ewing's basketball ability and Brown's coaching skill could not overcome injuries to Bill Cartright, Bernard King, James Bailey, and Pat Cummings, plus the contractual holdout of Louis Orr. Add to that the ejection of guard Darrell Walker in the second quarter and you understood when Brown moaned, "We were a bit short-handed tonight." In fact, after Ken Bannister and Bob Thornton fouled out, the Knicks had only seven players available at the end of their 110-96 loss to the Blazers. "The only way we could win was if everyone played perfect," said Brown.

Rarely does a team that has just lost its seventeenth straight regular season game receive such attention. But despite the media scrutiny, there was another story on the Knicks that eluded reporters. Away from the media crush, guard Butch Carter dressed quickly. This would be his last trip to the West Coast as a professional basketball player.

As Hubie Brown's press conference concluded, Carter slipped through the crowded hallway past the television truck that had just beamed the game back to the Big Apple, and exited into a cool rain. A bus was waiting to take the team to the airport for a short flight to Seattle, but Carter ignored it as I drove up. He tossed his equipment bag into the back seat and relaxed for the twenty-minute drive.

The veteran of six NBA seasons didn't have to apologize for his performance. He'd played 17 minutes, his longest stint of the season, but contributed only 3 points against 4 turnovers. Butch explained that the team had flown up from Los Angeles that morning, and since he'd not played the previous night against the Lakers, he'd pumped a stationary bicycle for thirty minutes to maintain his conditioning. "My legs were tired," he sighed. "But that's the way it goes. I'll get another opportunity."

When asked if this was really his last season, Butch said that yes, the decision was made. No matter what happened on the court, he was prepared to enter the business world full-time after the 1985-86 season. Though he didn't have much to show for the current season, he could look back on 360-plus games as a member of the Lakers, Pacers and Knicks. Three times he'd scored more than 40 points in a contest.

Butch had always been a good shooter. The 6'5" guard had earned a reputation as a clutch shot while playing for coach Bobby Knight at Indiana. He'd hit the winning basket in the waning seconds to give the Hoosiers the NIT title in 1979, and scored the decisive points in overtime to beat Ohio State for the Big Ten title in 1980. He'd also written his name into the NBA record book for the most points scored in an overtime period — 14 against Boston when he was a member of the Indiana Pacers.

So why was he ready to walk away from it all? Certainly things would improve on the Knicks with Ewing at the pivot. Wasn't there some motivation to stay around a little longer, to chase after a championship ring?

Butch laughed and talked about his two sons, three-year-old Brandon and newborn baby Blake. "When I got ready to go to training camp, Brandon said, 'Daddy, I don't want you going away and playing basketball no more.' "

"You mean he's not impressed with your NBA career?" I asked.

"No, Brandon is only impressed with French toast and pancakes." Butch was silent for a moment, and the only sounds were the rapid beat of the wiper blades and a constant swish of cars kicking up mist on the freeway. "I really miss the family. Last time I was home, Brandon and I sat on the back deck and lined up popcorn for the big gray squirrels that live in the woods behind us. Then I had to go back to the big city. . . . We have a peace and harmony at our house."

He told of the plan he and his wife, Jill, had developed. Both had their college degrees. Butch had studied marketing, and for the last two years, he'd carefully researched a business, put together a limited partnership, and opened three self-serve car washes in and around his hometown of Spring Valley, Ohio. His plan to own twenty-five car washes in ten years had significant profit potential.

Butch Carter was not one of the higher paid players in the league. He was sobered by a statistic he quoted from the NBA players association: "Five years after they're done playing, eighty percent of all NBA players are broke." He paused to let that thought sink in. "That's a staggering number. And the reason for it is that we get so caught up in our athletic ability that we don't realize that if we don't have some type of education or business to sustain our cash flow, we end up spending our savings."

As we turned onto the airport exit ramp, Butch began talking about his childhood in Middletown, Ohio. His father left home when Butch was twelve, and as the oldest of seven children, Butch had to assume responsibility for helping his mother. That's a major reason he wants to change careers. "It's not worth the money for me to run around the country playing basketball, and be away from my sons. I would like to think my life would have been a lot better if I'd had a father around to give me some guidance."

Actually his father did come around after Butch started earning accolades for his football and basketball skills. And when Butch signed his first NBA contract as a rookie with the Los Angeles Lakers, Dad asked Butch to co-sign a bank loan that would help him establish a small business. Application was made at two banks, and when one bank gave approval, Butch signed the note. He also made the down payment on a dream home before leaving for training camp.

We found a parking place and walked into the nearly deserted terminal. With an hour to spare before the team's flight, we found the coffee shop and sat in a far corner by the mall. To help me understand what he wanted to share, he related an experience with the Lakers. "Actually, it began in college," he explained. "Kent Benson (now of the Detroit Pistons) was the head of the Fellowship of Christian Athletes on campus. I went to some of the meetings with him, but I wasn't ready to make a commitment. It was more important that I be accepted by my friends and teammates. And since we practiced on Sundays, it was easy to skip church."

Butch was a second round draft choice for the Lakers, but for a while, there was some doubt whether he'd actually report. Because of his business degree, he'd already been offered a job with a major corporation. Only after he led the Lakers' summer league team in scoring, and the team agreed to guarantee his first year's salary, did he decide to try pro basketball.

Away from the discipline of home and college, Butch began to experience the ups and downs of life. When he got playing time and performed well, he felt great. When he rode the bench or played poorly, he was depressed. He was riding an emotional roller coaster. He relished his accomplishment and the adulation of his family, except that one grandmother was not impressed. "Everyone here is thrilled about you and how you play," she told him one day on the phone. "The only thing that would thrill me is if you would come to Christ."

That made Butch think. This woman was one person he *knew* cared about him, and the only thing that concerned her was his relationship with God. Butch understood what she meant, for he'd learned in church and through Lakers team chapel services that Christ had died for his sins, and after His resurrection had ascended into heaven, and would enter a person's life — if that person was willing. Butch finally surrendered to Christ in February, 1981, at 2:30 a.m. at the Hyatt Regency Hotel in Arlington, Virginia.

Immediately, Butch Carter's priorities changed and his emotions stabilized. "Instead of my priority being basketball, it was now going to heaven."

But his faith got an immediate test. As Butch picked at a slice of banana cream pie, he admitted that he had never revealed what he was about to say to a reporter. People had known that he had financial troubles, but he'd waited because the story had only recently seen its conclusion.

"I went home during All-Star break," Butch explained, relating what happened shortly after his conversion. "I discovered there was a lien against my house. It turned out that my dad was not repaying the loan."

The news got worse. Not only was Dad not paying back the one loan, but Butch's signature had been forged on another bank note as well. Butch was now liable for a whopping debt, and the interest was at two percent over prime, which at that time was twenty percent. "The interest that year was more than $18,000."

Butch confronted his father, who promised to catch up on his payments. But by summer, it was obvious that wasn't going to happen. In fact, Butch faced the prospect of losing his home if he didn't make the Lakers team that fall. Butch approached the banks to see if they would allow him to reschedule the payments, but instead they wanted to foreclose on his home. Even that wouldn't begin to pay off the enormous debt, so only one option remained — bankruptcy.

There are basically two forms of bankruptcy, and Butch is quick to say that he chose Chapter 13, which didn't forgive his debts. "You have to pay the money back," he explained. "But it keeps the creditors from hassling you. I started making payments of $1,000 a month to a trustee."

It wasn't a lot, but it was a start. During this time Butch married. The newlyweds had to place their faith in God, that somehow He would guide them through the financial mess. "There was no question that my faith told me I should pay the money back, and that, some-how, it would work out for the best." The couple agreed to live on a very tight budget. They moved into a small apartment and rented out their dream house, applying the rent money to the debt.

Butch and his wife began spending more time in Bible study, and in the Scriptures they learned some principles of money management. Things like tithing — giving at least ten percent of their income to the church, missionary work, and local charities. They learned to budget, and they learned of patience — that things take time. They even discovered that the Bible had a specific word about Butch's problem. "It is poor judgment to countersign another's note, to become responsible for his debts," he read in Proverbs 17:18 (Living Bible). It was one of five such warnings in Proverbs. "Jill and I actually thanked God it was happening now," he said. "I was only twenty-two years old. It wouldn't destroy us."

It took nearly four years to pay the money back. With a smile, Butch said that just three months ago, he'd made the final payment. "When we made that last payment, it was like seeing a sunrise after you've been trapped in a cave for a month." And his integrity had paid off as he started his new business. "My banker loves to hear from me," he said. "Right now, our account is bulging. He knows what I've gone through, and it's been a testimony to him that I paid it all back."

It was almost time to board the plane. We got up and passed Hubie Brown, who was eating a sandwich with one of his assistant coaches. As we paid our bill and headed into the lobby, Butch reflected on the lessons he'd learned through his trial. "You know, my father showed me what happens when you take the quick and easy way out. He quit my family, and didn't even think about what effect it had on his kids. He's done that all his life. It doesn't get you anywhere. I've learned that you only get out of life what you put into it."

He admitted that it was hard to forgive his father. He's still working through that process. But he also agrees that he's a stronger man today because he insisted on keeping his word. He's matured as a result and is respected in his hometown. Someday, his children will benefit, too, for they will see a father who persevered through tough times. "I've learned that we can always pray," he said as we parted. "Remember, our faith in Christ is the only thing that's going to last forever." In light of all that, prolonging an NBA career really isn't that important.

Author's note: Butch Carter was released by the Knicks shortly after our interview. Philadelphia signed him and he played with the Sixers for ten days before he was released again.

Gene Banks

9

BASKETBALL AND THE INTELLECTUAL
Gene Banks

"It's not what the instrument looks like; it's the note it plays and how well it blends in and helps create a melody."

Eugene L. Banks, Jr.
From his commencement address at
Duke University

Gene Banks is a muscular power forward who is justifiably proud of his basketball achievements. During his freshman year at Duke University, he led the Blue Devils to the NCAA finals. Three years later, he led the prestigious Atlantic Coast Conference in scoring and became an early second-round draft choice for the San Antonio Spurs. There he enjoyed four very productive seasons, averaging nearly 12 points per game while shooting a field goal percentage of better than 54 percent.

In spite of these and many other athletic accomplishments, Gene is far prouder of a moment that occurred off the court.

Gene's fifth NBA season was being spent in Chicago as a member of the Bulls, and he emphasized how pleased he was with the trade. "I had my differences with Coach Fitzsimmons," he said about the man who replaced Stan Albeck in San Antonio. "I knew if I stayed, my career was in jeopardy." In Chicago, Gene was reunited with Coach Albeck, along with two other former Spurs — George "the Iceman" Gervin, and John Paxson. Teamed with superstar Michael Jordan, they hoped to create a new NBA power.

But a discussion with Gene Banks does not have to center on basketball. This 225-pound gentleman is a well-rounded person who is constantly striving to increase his learning. It was appropriate that much of our conversation occurred in a hotel lounge decorated in a library motif. Surrounded by books, Gene Banks was in his favorite environment.

It's easy to look at athletes and think of them only in terms of statistics, awards, or team accomplishments. Unfortunately many athletes, pro and amateur, have neglected their intellectual development. They are unprepared for that inevitable moment of truth, when they must hang up the sneakers and enter the work force. There are others, however, who succeed in sports without sacrificing their future. Gene Banks is one such person.

This 6'8" forward isn't one to simply preach "hit the books" to school-age kids. He models it. Even after he graduated from college — in four years — he continued to stimulate his mind by reading, building his ever-growing library, and challenging himself to explore new areas of life and culture. "I just finished reading *Lincoln* by Gore Vidal," Gene said as he stretched his legs and sipped a Coke. "I enjoy reading books on history — the Civil War, reconstruction, black history. I also am interested in some of the new books about the Vietnam War. I read Henry Kissinger's memoirs and was interested in how he dealt with foreign policy. I wrote my senior thesis on that at Duke."

Presently, Gene reads three or four books each month, taking particular advantage of the time on airplanes. His library includes two sets of encyclopedias and about twenty dictionaries, plus a growing children's library he is developing for his children. "I take pride in my library. It gives me instant access to knowledge."

Gene's background was the type that has derailed many youngsters long before they reach college. He grew up in the inner city of Philadelphia. His parents were divorced when he was two years old and at various times he lived with his father, mother, and grandparents.

Most of the time he lived with his mother, who was a respiratory therapist, and stepfather. They endured the heartache of a daughter with spinal meningitis. Diagnosed at the age of two, she was not expected to live past her tenth birthday. She died at the age of nineteen. "That kept me from having a big head when I did well in basketball," Gene said.

Church was an important part of this family's life. In fact, after they moved out of the projects, church met in their family basement. It was a pentecostal group, consisting of family, cousins, and a few neighbors. "They called me the quiet one at church," Gene said with a laugh. "I would always observe but I never made a lot of noise because I didn't understand what was happening. Later I learned that these people worked so hard during the week, and this was a time for them to let out their joy. It was in church that I learned what true love was about."

And it was there, at the age of twelve, that Gene Banks gave his own life to Jesus Christ — "got saved" is what they called it. "We'd have these 'tarrying' services, and I didn't want to go to them because someone always got saved. My mom wanted me to get saved, but she told me it was my decision. I used to think people were faking it at these services — until I experienced it. It was an intense battle. I kept saying Jesus' name over and over, and then I'd have thoughts like, *You could have been with the guys; you could have been with your friends.* God won that battle."

Once Gene personally experienced the reality of Christ, he, too, got involved with church. His natural curiosity led to his studying Hebrew with his sisters. Until basketball practices started interfering, he continued the Hebrew studies for three years, in the process gaining a deep appreciation for the Old Testament.

As that Hebrew class demonstrates, Gene was already an inquisitive person with a desire to learn. But an experience during his senior year at West Philadelphia High School radically changed his life. He was a basketball star and a decent student, but he waited too long to finish a paper.

"It was a twenty-page paper," he said. "It was supposed to be typed, just like in college. A teammate of mine and I worked late that night, and then we went over to our friend Jackie's house and got her paper and tried to pick some things out of it. Well, we finally finished the paper but we used some of Jackie's stuff. And Jackie told the teacher."

The teacher was William H. Deadwyler, Jr. and he gave Gene Banks a private forty-minute lecture. For the next few months, Gene had to report to Mr. Deadwyler's classroom every day after school. He had to read a book each day, in addition to his regular school work. During those months, he read all of Shakespeare, learned how to fill out job applications, and was introduced to music by Mozart, Chopin, and Tchaikovsky. Gene cried more than once as his friends were out having a good time while he had to study. But the strict English teacher insisted, "Someday you will thank me."

Today, Gene is deeply grateful for those months of discipline. Gene's reading skills jumped dramatically, and his grades improved. "He'd get mad at me when I got a B because he wanted me to do more than just get by. The benefit was that when I graduated, I could attend any college I wanted." He chose Duke, a tough academic institution, where he majored in history and political science.

However, the transformation to dedicated student wasn't complete, for Gene had his lackadaisical moments. And that's where another person, Dean Virginia Bryan, challenged him. "Just because you're a ballplayer doesn't mean anything," she told Gene. "I see a lot of promise in you, a lot of intelligence, but you're wasting it. If you keep it up, you won't stay in this school."

Gene loved Duke with its beautiful campus, social and cultural opportunities, and academic atmosphere. When a team from the now-defunct American Basketball Association tried to induce him to turn pro after his freshman year, Gene refused. Instead, he learned how to use the library, and became a master at all-night marathon study sessions.

"They called me Mr. Clutch!" he said with a laugh. "I really enjoyed it when I began *understanding* things. I could sit down with my peers and speak intelligently about different political theories and understand the concept of social structure. Just like basketball, I learned to study by practice. And once I could read and understand what I was reading, school became a joy."

And from that discipline came his most significant achievement. It had nothing to do with his athletic accomplishments; he earned this honor in competition with other senior students at the university. It was the chance to deliver the commencement address during graduation ceremonies at Duke. His message was titled, "I Believe in Music":

> ". . . We must learn the culture of each of our instruments, appreciating them in their differences and learning to blend them so that, like a symphony, we produce harmony. In our future steps, when we venture into our professions, remember the music that was played here at Duke University and blend it to that needed symphony in your profession.
>
> "Our symphony has ended, but we can all become parts of new, different symphonies — symphonies that can grow and join until we are all part of the same symphony again, a larger, better one . . . a world of harmony. Duke can be the place where this began.
>
> "Again, it's not what the instrument looks like; it's the note it plays and how well it blends in and helps create a melody. . . ."

The passionate oration received a standing ovation, and after the ceremony Gene's mother, Mr. Deadwyler, and Virginia Bryan joined in a communal hug. "I cried," Gene admitted. "I'm the first from my family to go to college and get a degree. And these people pushed me. I still get tears thinking about it."

Gene is so passionate about his convictions that sometimes he has to restrain himself and realize that others haven't arrived where he is. He admitted that sometimes he's pushed his children too hard, but he's learning the balance. He told about the comic books he's collecting. "It's a good way to start kids reading, because they like the pictures. At one time, books without pictures intimidated me. But I encourage kids to take the challenge. Once you've mastered books with pictures, try something else. In basketball you have coaches who can help you. Well, if you have trouble reading, there are parents, teachers, tutors, friends. If there is a word you don't know, you can look it up. So you don't have to feel ashamed.

"Take Shakespeare, for example. At first, I was intimidated by all the 'thees and thous.' Then I began to see beyond the old language style and I discovered why Shakespeare was so great. His plays aren't that difficult. Some of them are very funny, and you learn a lot of lessons about people and life. One of my favorites is *Richard III*. You see the most basic elements of life when Richard says, 'A horse! A horse! My kingdom for a horse!' Why did he say that? Because when his life was threatened, nothing else mattered."

Gene is not afraid to try new experiences. He's traveled to China and Russia ("basketball has opened a lot of doors") and enjoys learning about different cultures. He speaks Spanish, some French and Hebrew — though he admits he's a little rusty. "You can understand people better when you understand their culture. Could you imagine if everyone were the same? God has made it so much fun, but many people don't realize how much fun it is. Someday I'd like to get a job with the government that would put me in contact with many different cultures."

Through his experience, Gene has developed some suggested study habits for young achievers:

1. Challenge a friend to "spelling games" from a dictionary or reading text.
2. If you have a boyfriend or girlfriend, read to each other. It aides your friendship and helps you succeed in school.
3. Choose a book that interests you and as you read, pretend you are one of the characters. This will help you better understand what the author is trying to say.
4. Use music to help relax you, or to pump yourself up for the assignment ahead.
5. Concentrate on basics such as math, science, and social studies. You will learn concepts that will help you in whatever profession you choose.
6. Get a library card, and use it.
7. Join a book club in order to help build your own personal library at a reasonable price.
8. Set personal goals and place them before you where you will see them every day.
9. Practice makes perfect. One must practice reading and writing. Learn to express yourself on paper.
10. Allow parents and teachers to help you reach your academic goals. They want you to achieve success, so when they push you, realize it's because they're concerned. Someday you'll thank them.

Gene's wife, Belle, has also achieved academic success. She is a graduate of North Carolina A & T. "She's a television producer," he said with a proud smile. "Now that she's pregnant, she won't do as much for a while.

But in San Antonio, she produced our team's half-time features. She's a great editor and taught me how to edit film."

The basketball player-intellectual admits he's not an easy person to live with, that there is a part of him he likes to keep to himself. He's had to adjust to marriage, and the faith that began during his childhood is a crucial element in that. In the Banks' home is a plaque of praying hands that reminds Gene and Belle of the source of their commitment to each other.

Perhaps the most consistent part of Gene's life is his basketball performance. Just as he went up and down in school, he admits that he has ups and downs spiritually. "It's because I don't have good practice habits," he said. "You can't wait for Sunday to go to church; you have to apply your faith every day. There are times when my mind will be on Jesus all day. And then there are times when I don't think about Him at all.

"But I'm so thankful to Him. I love life. I have so much to be appreciative of. God has truly shown me His goodness."

"When one believes him/herself to be smart, he/she has taken the first step. When one puts forth the effort to become smart, he/she has taken the second and most important step toward academic achievement.

". . . for God so loved the world that He gave His only Son as a sacrifice for the betterment of man's foolheartedness. And God so loved the world that He gave man his own mind to develop and gain knowledge."

Eugene L. Banks, Jr.

Ed Rush

10

ONE DAY IN THE LIFE
OF AN NBA REF
Ed Rush

Ed Rush had made this walk so many times he could do it in his sleep. The United Airlines flight from Los Angeles had just landed at Sea-Tac International Airport. Carrying a small black suitcase and a garment bag, Ed deplaned and walked briskly into the terminal, rode down the escalator, passed the baggage claim area, and stopped in front of a colorful phone board displaying more than thirty local hotels. Within five minutes, Ed and his partner, Jim Capers, were riding one of the

Airport Marriott's red vans. Fifteen minutes after landing, Ed was settled into his home for the next twenty-four hours.

Rush and Capers are NBA referees, and this was their third stop in as many days. Wednesday night they'd worked a Utah-Portland game in Salt Lake City; Thursday it was the Lakers and Phoenix in the Forum; tonight it would be the Sonics and Clippers in Seattle Center Coliseum.

For twenty years, such rigorous schedules have been routine for Ed Rush. Since 1966, when at the age of twenty-four he became the youngest referee in league history, Ed has refined his travel logistics to a system that would make any travel agent proud. In the same way, he has studied and practiced to master every rule and technique in an attempt to one day call a "perfect game."

Sports cannot function without umpires, judges, and referees. While every sport presents a unique challenge, officials in professional basketball may face the ultimate test. With the phenomenal increase in the size, speed, quickness, and overall athletic ability of professional basketball players who compete within the limited space of ninety-four-by-fifty-foot courts, referees have had to improve, also. "If we don't get better every year, we're in trouble," Ed said as he picked up the phone to confirm lunch with two friends.

The National Basketball Association has worked hard to develop the finest officials. The league's program is a model for professional sports. Hundreds of applicants compete for a handful of openings. The top candidates, along with minor league officials and lower-rated NBA officials, attend classes and officiate games in several summer leagues throughout the United States. The most promising newcomers work in the Continental Basketball Association.

After several years of minor league and summer league experience, the best refs are promoted to the NBA where they find the rigors even tougher. In nearly every NBA game, officials are graded on a one-hundred-point scale in areas such as rule interpretations, floor mechanics, hand signals, self control, judgment calls, dealing with coaches and players, overall professionalism, and concentration over forty-eight minutes. Only the highest-rated officials work playoff games. Referees spend off-days studying video tapes of their games, sometimes under the direction of chief of officiating staff Darell Garretson. In the heat of an intense game, it's easy for fans to forget that NBA referees have done everything humanly possible to get every call right.

Below Ed's room in the hotel's atrium was a pool, and beside it a huge buffet: salads, seafood, a rack of beef, fresh fruit, and a selection of deserts. Since it was seven-and-a-half hours to game time, Ed was ready for the spread.

As we headed downstairs, he admitted that most good college officials could referee pro games technically. "The toughest part about working in the NBA is not calling the plays, but dealing with the personalities. Put an inexperienced ref in the Boston Garden for a Lakers-Celtics game — with all those banners and 15,000 screaming fans and the television cameras — he'd be awe-struck. You have to make the transition from being a fan to being an official. I'm not a basketball fan. I think we have a great game, but I'm a football and baseball fan."

Ed lunched with Ron Coder, an ex-NFL and USFL offensive lineman who played in Ed's hometown of Philadelphia, and George Toles, a Seattle businessman who doubles as public address announcer for the Sonics.

Afterward, Ed reclined on his bed and reminisced about the start of his career. "I began refereeing basketball when I was in ninth grade, about the time I realized I was not a very good player. I reffed our high school team's scrimmages and earned $10 each Saturday doing Biddy Basketball games. In college, I picked up $75 to $100 a week reffing games almost every night of the week. After graduation I started working college games.

"Back then, there weren't many men applying to ref in the NBA. The salary and benefits weren't nearly what they are today. The league recruited me. They liked my youth, the fact that I was teachable, and that I didn't mind traveling. They were willing to take five years to mold me into a strong pro official."

Today, Ed is not the same man as that brash young twenty-four-year-old who covered his insecurity with an arrogant exterior. If a coach or player questioned a call, Ed responded with put-downs. He could argue and swear as well or better than any player. Though his

style worked, today Ed Rush is a far better referee —
without the cockiness and swearing. He still "controls"
a game, but with a confident assurance that comes from
twenty-plus years of experience and a spiritual maturity.
In fact, he can even admit that he's not perfect, something
the old Ed Rush never did.

While still grueling, an NBA ref's life is more stream-
lined now. The thirty full-time referees work in crews
of six, and pairings are usually made between a veteran
and a new or less-experienced ref. The pairings rotate
every few weeks, and a schedule of game assignments
is issued once a month. Each ref can expect to travel
approximately two weeks out of every four.

Refs are required to be in the city where they will
work the night before each game, unless they're working
two consecutive nights. Then they must take the first
flight out in the morning to their next assignment. That's
an important rule: If they miss or skip the first flight
and then can't make their destination for any reason,
they're $1,000 poorer. To prevent that, Ed always uses
a travel alarm to back up a hotel's wake-up call.

At 3 P.M., Ed slipped into bed for his pre-game nap.
He was asleep within two minutes and awoke shortly
before 5 P.M. He dressed in coat and tie, checked the
contents of his equipment bag, and shortly before 6
o'clock headed up the freeway in a rented car. He
passed the Kingdome, the home of the Sonics for the
past six seasons, and continued to the grounds of the .
1963 World's Fair. The Space Needle, sporting Christmas

lights, loomed above the Seattle Center Coliseum, home of the Sonics for the first eleven years of their existence.

The dressing room for officials was located down a long tunnel, nearly one-hundred yards from the court, opposite the visitor's dressing room. Walking down that long corridor brought back memories of the old Ed Rush who often jawed with coaches and players in that tunnel. He stopped to visit with Bob Blackburn, the Sonics' radio play-by-play voice during the franchise's eighteen-year existence. "One of the best games I ever saw here was one where you worked alone," Bob recalled.

Ed remembered: "It was between these same two teams. My partner was fogged in at San Francisco."

Jim Capers arrived shortly after Ed, an hour before game time. Though he's reffed professional basketball for fourteen years, Jim is better known as the brother of Virginia Capers, a Tony Award-winning actress. As the two began to change into their navy blue slacks, gray jerseys, and black Converse shoes, they talked about the upcoming contest between the Sonics and Clippers. Good communication is essential for a referee team, so pre-game discussion always focuses on basketball. Talk often covers individual players in order to help refs anticipate potential problems.

Ed jogged in place, then did some stretching exercises on the floor to loosen his back, which had endured two operations in the past five years. "Have you had the Clippers this year?" he asked Jim.

"A few weeks ago. They do a lot of hand checks. Both sides do. You've got to watch Nixon, Sobers, Henderson."

Ed hadn't worked a Sonics game this season and wanted to know about Seattle's defense. "Do they trap?"

"Some. But not as much as the Clippers."

"What about their first round draft choice, Xavier McDaniel?"

"Watch him," Jim warned. "He's very aggressive on the offensive boards."

Ed grabbed a case book — a series of questions and answers issued every year along with the updated rule book. It helps officials review every conceivable situation they might face on the floor. "If you call a foul away from the play in the last two minutes or overtime, what do you do?"

Jim correctly answered that anyone in the game may attempt the free throw for the offended team, which also retains possession. The ball is then inbounded nearest the point where play was suspended.

"I had to call that last year in Kansas City, against the Clippers," Ed recalled. "No one understood what was happening."

As Jim wrapped his right thigh, Ed asked, "What if a player on each team is injured at the same time?"

"If no one calls time out, play continues," Jim answered. "Let's talk about floor mechanics."

Ed grabbed a wonder slate, one of those erasable pads used by kids. The two reviewed their positions on the floor in various situations, to insure that both men would not be watching the ball at the same time. "That's one of the hard adjustments for NBA refs," Ed explained. "We've grown up watching the ball. But many of the fouls occur away from the ball."

Another adjustment was the result of the NBA's one-year experiment with three officials. "We had much better angles then," Ed said. "Now that we're back to two, we've tried to retain some of those same angles." One way that's done is by having the trail ref, who works above the key, watch the post play under the basket while the lead ref, who's often blocked out by the giants in the middle, watches the corners.

As a knock on the locker room door informed the men that it was time to make their appearance, Ed reminded Jim to make a good toss to start the game. It would cost Ed ten bucks if his partner made a poor toss on a jump ball and Ed didn't blow the whistle.

The Sonics used to average more than twenty thousand fans per game in their glory years in the Kingdome, but tonight there were barely five thousand on hand. Ed wouldn't let that affect his performance. He reminded himself that every player was a highly paid professional who deserved the referee's best effort. He knew that Seattle was struggling to regain their winning ways under new coach Bernie Bickerstaff while L. A. coach Don Chaney's job was in jeopardy after his team had suffered

several lopsided defeats. With that incentive, L. A. jumped to an early twelve-point lead, only to see it shrink
to five by the end of the first quarter. Their lead lasted
until 5:21 remained in the half. At halftime, Seattle had
taken command, 55-48.

"That's the hardest half we've had on this trip," said
Ed during halftime intermission. "There's no flow to it."

Jim agreed. "We have to remain aggressive inside.
Don't start back too quick in the trail position."

As Seattle began to pull away in the second half,
L. A. became increasingly frustrated. Coach Chaney
complained bitterly after Ed made a traveling call on
Michael Cage. Center Kurt Nimphius fell to his knees
to protest Jim's foul call as Seattle's Jack Sikma completed
a three-point play. Norm Nixon tried to get Ed to call a
foul on Sonic guard Al Wood, then protested an out-of-
bounds call.

With less than five minutes left in the game, Nimphius
complained again and drew a technical foul. Jamaal
Wilkes' three-point shot at the buzzer cut Seattle's victory
margin to 19 points.

Back in their dressing room, Jim and Ed devoured
sandwiches and completed their post-game paperwork.
Jim had to report on the technical. "I told Nimphius
that if he complained again, I'd have to call a 'T.' He
said, 'Just go ahead and call it now.' So I did."

Ed said that Nixon complained when L. A. was down
by 20, wondering if Seattle had any fouls. "I told him
he should worry more about playing his man." A review

of the box score showed that Seattle was whistled for 25 fouls, the Clippers for 23. About Chaney's protest, Ed admitted he might have made the wrong call. "I'd like to see a video of that."

After they showered and dressed, two policemen escorted the refs from the arena. The parking lot was empty, except for a couple of Sonic players walking to their cars, pursued by autograph seekers. "See you in Chicago!" said Jim, who was meeting some friends for a post-game dinner. Their next assignment was in four days.

It was now 11 P.M. as Ed headed onto the freeway for the twenty-minute drive back to the hotel. As he took the airport exit, Ed passed the Holiday Inn where the most memorable moment of his career — indeed, his entire life — occurred.

"I'll never forget it," he said. "It was 11:30 at night on October 5, 1979."

Ed was eager to talk about that experience as we were seated in the Marriott's dining room. After asking the waiter to leave a pitcher of water, Ed explained the context of that historic moment. "To say the least, I wasn't very mature when I started reffing in the NBA. I got into a helter-skelter lifestyle that included a lot of partying and looking constantly for materialistic gain.

"What confused me was that every time I attained something, the satisfaction lasted only about twenty-four hours. I felt like there was a constant leak in my life, I never achieved total satisfaction. As my career progressed and my salary increased, the temptations also increased and my lust for materialistic things became greater."

Two events caused him to stop and evaluate his life. One was a serious back operation that put his career in jeopardy. The other was a divorce. "My wife and kids left me because I never had much time for them. With those two setbacks, I started thinking about what was really important in life."

Ed recovered from his operation and reported for the 1979 pre-season training camp where he roomed with veteran referee Bernie Fryer. "Bernie's background was very similar to mine. But I saw a change in his life, and I started to ask him questions. He told me he had accepted Christ as his personal Savior.

"Usually during exhibition games, we work with different officials each night. This year, however, Bernie and I were paired for all six games. Our final pre-season game was in Seattle and after the game, George Toles and Norm Evans, an NFL lineman with the Seahawks, visited Bernie and me in the locker room. I knew they believed the same as Bernie. They suggested we pray together. So we stood in a circle and clasped hands and prayed. And as we did, I felt a presence in the room — what I thought must be God. An overwhelming peace came over me and left me speechless."

That night, back at his hotel room, Ed reviewed his past and the events of the last few weeks, and wound up on his knees next to his bed. "I gave up and said, 'Christ, I'm Yours. I've failed.' Even though society looked

at me as a success, I knew in my heart I had not suc-
ceeded. Though I didn't understand what was happening,
I knew I was going to change."

At first, Ed continued to use the same combative
style that had made him successful for fourteen years.
Every objection by a player or coach was cause for an
expletive-not-deleted reaction as Ed fought to maintain
control. But as he started learning and talking about
his faith, he found that his approach contradicted the
ways of Christ.

It came to a head in Madison Square Garden in
March of 1980. "Earlier that day I had been telling a
close Philadelphia friend about my personal walk with
God. That night I was working a game between the
Knicks and 76ers. In the middle of the third quarter I
got into an argument with Darryl Dawkins. I went right
after him with profanity. In the midst of this dialogue,
I looked down on the floor and saw a TV technician with
a boom mike pointed right at me. Instantly, I realized
my hypocrisy. I knew I had to make a change."

That was a fearful transition, one which made Ed
wonder if he might have to quit his profession. As the
1980-81 season started, he determined that he would
attempt to work each game in a non-arrogant fashion,
trying to honor God while he was on the floor. He wondered if the players and coaches might see the change,
and take advantage of him.

In fact, the opposite happened. He wound up with
his highest rating ever, worked the most playoff games
of his career, and was slated to work game seven of the

championship series, had Boston not won the title in game six.

Today, Ed Rush is a totally different man. His personal life rebounded with his marriage to Linda, a former flight attendant for Republic Airlines, and the birth of their first child, Jeff. The NBA has provided a good living for Ed Rush, and he is using his success to help others less fortunate. He teaches a class for basketball referees in a Philadelphia prison, where reffing is the highest paying job. He already has one graduate living in a halfway house and working high school games.

On the road, he often uses off days to conduct referee clinics for Prison Fellowship, an organization started by Charles Colson of Watergate fame. After a couple of hours of teaching and coaching, he casually tells those who are interested about his Christian faith. "I'm always on a high after I leave the prisons."

Ed had finished his second pitcher of water, downed a full meal — topped off by a dish of Haagen Daaz rum raisin ice cream — and talked for nearly two hours. As he headed up to his room, he concluded that he had the greatest job in the world: "There's no other job I'd rather have in professional sports. It's a challenge to know that I represent the integrity of pro basketball. I don't have to worry about whether I won or lost. I just have to look in the mirror and know I was fair, that I did the best job possible."

He stopped at the door of his room. "I'd like to work another ten years, but I would never do this just for money. Every year I want to see how I feel as the

new season approaches." In a few hours Ed would fly
home to Philadelphia for two days. Then he would
board another plane and stay in another hotel. "Right
now, I'm already looking forward to next week. Chicago-
Boston, then Milwaukee-Lakers the next night. Two
good ones in a row!"

Kelvin Ransey

11

HEEDING THE CALL

Kelvin Ransey

The sound of a single basketball bouncing against the Memorial Coliseum court reverberated throughout the empty arena. New Jersey coach Dave Wohl was conducting rehearsal for the game that night against Portland. Net guard Kelvin Ransey, a former member of the Trail Blazers, was playing the role of Portland's starting point guard against the Nets' front line defense.

For forty-five minutes, the Nets ran half-speed through all the possible offensive and defensive combinations they could expect from their opponents. Through this process, Wohl hoped his team could pull out their first road victory of the year after seven defeats. The Nets weren't that bad a team; they'd won all six of their home games. But they needed some road wins if they hoped to challenge Boston and Philadelphia in the Eastern Conference.

With rehearsal completed, Wohl divided the squad into four teams of three for shooting games. Two teams squared off at each end of the court, competing to be the first to score fifteen baskets from each of three locations, beginning at the foul line and finishing at the baseline. After the first round, the victors squared off at the north end and Coach Wohl offered $25 per man to the winners.

In a sport where the average salary is in six figures, $25 doesn't seem like much incentive. But Kelvin, Buck Williams, and Otis Birdsong competed against Mike O'Koren, Darryl Dawkins and Bobby Cattage as if this were for the NBA title. After each shot, the shooter scrambled to recover the ball and whipped it to the next man in line. With assistant coach Paul Silas announcing the score from underneath the basket, the O'Koren-Dawkins-Cattage crew jumped to a seven-point lead. But the Ransey-Williams-Birdsong squad battled back and needed just one final score to win. All three players missed, allowing O'Koren to finally hit the winning jumper. Practice concluded with a round of free throws as the six combatants savored the contest like they would a fine meal.

"We needed that to help us relax," said Kelvin Ransey as he shook hands with his old friend, Al Egg, a few moments later. "But Otis let us down!" he laughed.

They were interrupted by Mychal Thompson shouting, "Hey Butter!" The Blazers were coming on the court for their morning shoot-around. It was Mychal who had given Kelvin that nickname, claiming that the guard was "smoother than Mrs. Butterworth's syrup."

After a brief visit with Mychal, Kelvin chatted with Portland coach Jack Ramsey, for whom Kelvin had enjoyed his finest years in the league. Portland had acquired Kelvin Ransey from Chicago after the Bulls made him the number four pick in the 1980 draft. He showed enough to miss winning Rookie-of-the-Year honors by a single vote. In two years with the Blazers, he led the team in assists — ranking among the NBA's top ten — while averaging nearly 16 points per game. During their brief conversation, Coach Ramsey told the New Jersey guard that he was sorry the Blazers had traded him.

As Portland began their workout, Kelvin and Al Egg headed for lunch. At a hotel coffee shop, Kelvin told his close friend that this might be his final season. "I'm going into the ministry," he announced. "I'm preaching my first sermon in three weeks!"

Al and Kelvin had met during Ransey's years in Portland. "You're like a brother to me," said Kelvin.

"When I lived here, I wasn't where I should have been spiritually. But you never stopped praying for me."

It was Kelvin who had originally suggested that Al, who was a leader in the local Fellowship of Christian Athletes, begin a chapel service before Blazers home games. At times, those chapels consisted only of Kelvin and Al. But gradually they grew and players on the visiting teams began attending along with Blazers such as Mychal Thompson.

Kelvin grew up in a strong Christian family that attended the Pentecostal church every Sunday. "My father said I could miss church any time he did," he likes to say, "but he never missed." With that heritage, an older brother and sister are now in the ministry.

Al and Kelvin ordered large bowls of seafood chowder. The soup arrived, full of large chunks of fish. Along with several slices of sourdough bread, it made for a surprisingly filling meal. While they ate, Kelvin admitted that despite his upbringing, he struggled in Portland. "In my background, I was taught to be consecrated, which means to be in touch with the Lord at all times — to study His Word, to know His will. But as I did well in basketball I stopped studying the Bible and I wouldn't pray. It was like I was caught in a tug of war."

Al recalled the trade that sent Kelvin to Dallas in June of 1982. "I remember you called me from Ohio and we cried and prayed together over the phone. You told me that you couldn't see it at the time, but God had to have a purpose for you being in Dallas."

"That's right, and He did!" Kelvin answered. "I wasn't very happy with things there. I didn't have a lot of playing time, and I began to see that basketball was just a business. I was just a piece of property. I never felt I got a fair shake with the Mavericks, but it drove me to a stronger relationship with Christ, which I now see as much more important. I started decreasing as far as basketball, but my spiritual life began to increase. And that's continued ever since."

"And God also had someone He wanted you to help."

"Mark Aguirre. We used to kid each other a lot. Mark had come to Christ the year before, and we got really close. He would come over after games and my wife would bake cookies. We'd sit and eat cookies, and we'd open the Bible and discuss things. On the road, we talked a lot. When I think of Dallas I remember our talks more than anything."

"And then came your trade to New Jersey."

"I prayed for a trade, hopefully to a place where I could regain the status I'd had in Portland. But I think the Nets only wanted me as security in case Micheal Ray Richardson couldn't overcome his drug problems."

"I believe it was right before the season that your dad died."

It was obvious that Kelvin still held a special memory for his father. Quietly, with deep feeling, he said, "My father was a great man. I never ever saw him curse, or drink, or smoke. He never raised his voice at my mother. He was a rock in the church.

"My father taught me how to work. He was a truck driver for a steel company. He also owned a dump truck and had a little business on the side. We'd often work with him, like when he had to clean up a place. Dad made sure it was spotless when we were done. 'If you do good work, they'll call you back,' he'd say. He was a great example."

That example was one of the motivations leading Kelvin to prepare for the ministry. "I got a feeling this past September, a deep gut feeling that God has a job for me to do. It was like He was saying it was time for me to let people know that God is the Savior of the world."

"So will this be your last year?" Al asked.

"I think so, but I'm not ruling ball out completely. The important thing is that I use my time in pro ball to prepare for the ministry. I'm studying a lot. I'll be giving my first sermon at my home church in Toledo, and then there's a minister in New Jersey who's lining up some speaking engagements for me."

"What's your sermon about?"

"A motivating hope!" A big smile lit up Kelvin's face. "The Lord gave me that message almost as soon as I accepted His call. I want to convey to people that they have a hope, no matter what they're going through. It's not like earthly hope that is always coupled with doubt. Our Christian hope is knowing, without any question, that as long as we're in the will of God, we will have His very best."

"You've changed a lot since the last time we talked," Al Egg observed. The eastern teams only visit western cities once during the regular season, so Al and Kelvin hadn't seen each other for nearly a year. "You just wanted to play as long as possible then."

"You're right. But when God speaks, I've got to listen."

"You're going to miss basketball?"

"My desires are changing. I think I'll miss the relationships with my teammates more than anything. I definitely won't miss the travel. Or the temptations."

"Are you going to pastor a church, or be an evangelist?"

"I think eventually I'll be going to different places, preaching. I'll go wherever the Lord leads me. I really want people to try the Lord, to get to know Him. So many people think you have to give up things, but they don't realize what they're gaining. The Bible says, 'Oh taste and see that the Lord is good.' It's like an ice cream cone. You can tell me it's good, but unless I taste it, I don't know. I want people to try the Lord and see how great He is!"

Al laughed at Kelvin's enthusiasm. "That's right on! You'll make a great preacher."

Before heading back to the hotel, Kelvin arranged for Al to meet with some of the Nets players for chapel later that afternoon. Then he settled into his room for a few hours of study. His athletic bag was stuffed with books — three different Bibles, a Bible handbook, a couple of commentaries, and a biography of Martin Luther King titled *Let the Trumpet Sound.* "I try to fill my mind with good things; I enjoy reading," he explained.

That night, the Nets showed a lot of good things on the court. Portland grabbed a quick six-point advantage, but New Jersey battled right back and had their first lead at 22-20 when Kelvin entered the game, replacing Otis Birdsong. With both Richardson and Ransey in the backcourt, the Nets demonstrated crisp ball movement and kept finding the open man for easy shots. The Nets had an eight-point lead by the end of the first quarter.

Early in the second period, Kelvin hit a sixteen-foot jumper. Then a teammate stripped the ball from Mychal Thompson and drove for a layup. Ransey immediately stole the ball from Steve Colter and fed O'Koren for a three-point basket. Before Portland could score again, New Jersey had run off 12 straight points. The Blazers never led again as the Nets gained their first road victory of the year, 108-102.

Coach Wohl had seen world champions make many similar runs as an assistant coach for the Lakers. He was pleased with the night's effort. "We pushed the ball up court. We moved the ball very well. We kept our spacing offensively. We executed and found the open man. That's what builds momentum."

As Kelvin dressed, he admitted that there was still a special feeling about playing in Portland. "I have fond memories of when I played here. I suppose it helps when you win."

Though Kelvin had contributed to the overall team effort, it wasn't necessarily reflected in his statistics — 17 minutes, 3 for 6 shooting, 1 assist, 1 steal, 7 points. But Kelvin wasn't concerned. That's an important lesson he's learned over the years. "A lot of times you play good defense and it doesn't show up in the stats. Or you make a good pass that leads to another pass, which leads to a score . . . you don't get an assist.

"Statistics don't mean that much to me any more. I'm not so concerned with my minutes or how many points I get; I'm more concerned with souls. I know that if I'm playing one hundred percent, that's the best I can do. I try to convey that to other players; statistics don't change me. Whether I score twenty points or two, I have to know I gave my best."

On this night, Kelvin's best was good enough.

Terry Cummings

12

THE RELATIONSHIP BEHIND THE STAR
Terry Cummings

Terry Cummings likes it when the game is on the line. He wants the ball in the game's final minutes and he goes for it by battling for the big defensive rebound, or forcing a bad pass, or tipping the ball on the offensive boards until he can control it. And, of course, he shoots.

When Terry Cummings' game is right, he soars above his NBA peers, cocking the ball high above his head and releasing an almost unblockable jump shot. Or he takes a quick step and blasts past a defender to the basket, usually drawing a foul and a chance for a three-point play. Or he hangs under the basket after garnering an offensive rebound and extends his long arms until he finds an opening for a layup.

The night prior to our meeting in Seattle, Terry had soared and scored 12 of his game-high 27 points in the fourth quarter, leading Milwaukee to another NBA win and a step closer to their seventh straight division title. "That's his third good game in a row," Bucks coach Don Nelson had told reporters after the game. "He was sensational tonight."

One can look at Terry Cummings' record and learn that he was the second pick of the 1982 NBA draft, became the first rookie since Kareem Abdul-Jabbar to rank among the top ten in both scoring and rebounding, has maintained 23.4 points-per-game career scoring average, scored 17 points in the 1985 NBA All-Star game and 41 points against Philadelphia in one playoff game.

But if all you know about this 6'9" forward for the Milwaukee Bucks are his stats, then you do not know Terry Cummings. To understand this man from Chicago's south side, you must know about the relationship that dominates his life.

Terry Cummings was born in Hammond, Indiana, the fifth of thirteen children. While he was an infant, the family moved to Chicago where his father worked in a smelting factory and did odd jobs as a handyman, garbage remover, garage attendant, and mechanic. Later, Mr. Cummings worked for the city as a maintenance employee. The pressures of providing for a large family left little time for the kids, so Terry had to grow up on his own.

Sports was an obvious release. "My first love was hockey," he admits. His idol was Chicago Black Hawk star Stan Mikita. But when Terry grew five inches in one summer, hockey was finished. "I knew my parents couldn't afford to buy skates to fit my feet."

So basketball became the natural alternative. He starred at Carver High School, then played three seasons at DePaul University. His coach, the venerable Ray Meyer, remembers him as an intense, hard-working player. "We used to have business people watch practice, and I would ask them, 'If you were going to hire one player off this team, who would it be?' They'd always say, 'Terry Cummings. Anybody who works that hard is going to be a success at anything he does.' "

Credit Ray Meyer for helping to convince Terry to stay in basketball. After a disappointing sophomore season, Terry was ready to quit the sport for more important matters. It had to do with his true calling in life. That relationship. Meyer helped Terry see that basketball and the relationship could co-exist. Cummings went on to have a spectacular junior season, after which he applied for early membership in the NBA.

The San Diego Clippers took him, then hesitated to pay the going rate for the league's number two draft choice. After sitting out the first five games, Terry signed a four-year contract, of which only one year was guaranteed. That's almost unheard of among premiere athletes, but Terry has a logical explanation: "The only thing that could keep me from playing was an injury. Otherwise, I make the team. So I didn't feel I was taking a big risk. However, because this is a business, I did take additional insurance on myself."

Those two years in San Diego were spectacular, but not necessarily pleasant. Terry led the team in all the important statistical categories, but with little support from his teammates, the Clippers were a last place team without a future. So Terry was elated when a trade sent him to Milwaukee in a six-player deal.

Coach Nelson was happy to acquire the power forward, but didn't realize Terry's full potential: "We knew he was big and strong and talented, but he'd never learned how to play." Nelson guided, yelled at and drilled Terry to make him a more complete player who fit into a system that emphasizes defense and passing above individual play.

"I always have some complaints about his defense," says Nelson. "But Terry passes the ball, dominates the boards, and makes the big shots. He's a sensational player, and we hope to make him even better."

But even sensational players have times when things don't go right. Like a 2-of-16 shooting night. During a recent season's first ten games, Terry had suffered through the first extended slump of his career. The horrific shooting night marked the first time in more than 230 NBA contests that he'd fail to score in double figures. That trial revealed elements of the real Terry Cummings.

Terry stepped off an elevator in the Seattle Sheraton wearing a bright blue DePaul sweat shirt and jeans. We strolled into the hotel's glass-enclosed restaurant. The sun had just set and rush-hour traffic was crawling outside on streets dampened by a Northwest drizzle. After the waitress took our order, Terry revealed that in the first game of the season, while leaping for a rebound, he was knocked to the floor. "I hit my knees flat on the floor," he reported matter-of-factly. "I never told Coach how much I was hurting. You get paid to do a job, and you go out and do it. That doesn't mean you always feel like doing it when you're hurt. But you do it anyway."

A reporter had asked Terry if he was frustrated by his ten-game slump. Terry had said no, that he was trying to remember that adversity is a learning experience. And just what had he learned? "I learned that when everything is going well for you, everyone jumps on your wagon. But when the wheels get chipped and the horseshoes bent, people start getting off. Still, you have to go on no matter how you feel.

"The Bible teaches that pride comes before a downfall, and humility before honor. This was a time to examine myself before God, which is something I do quite often. During hard times I learn more about Terry, more about God, more about love and friendship and mercy — things I wouldn't learn unless God humbled me."

Terry doesn't intend to forget those lessons. He writes them down in notebooks and refers to them often. It's

one way to keep that relationship alive and fresh and
vibrant. It wasn't always so.

Before the relationship, Terry's life revolved around
the streets of Chicago. Relatively speaking, he wasn't
the worst kid in the neighborhood. He broke into a few
cars and trucks, smoked cigarettes, dabbled briefly with
drugs, carried a pistol and knife, did a little shoplifting,
a little fighting.

"When you're in the jungle, you tend to act like
Tarzan if you want to survive," he explained. "I really
thought it was fun." Today, many of his former street
friends are hopelessly addicted to drugs. Or in jail. Or
dead. Even as a teenager, Terry recognized the danger,
but he didn't know there was an alternative until one
night, when he had a dream so vivid that it changed
his life.

When he was sixteen years old, Terry was spending
a few summer weeks with his grandmother in Hammond,
Indiana. After playing basketball in the street, he fell
into an exhausted sleep. He describes the dream: "At
first, it was like the roof of the house had disappeared
and I could see the sky. And in the sky, I saw the
clouds split open. Then I saw a man on a white horse.
He was dressed in white and wore a crown and there
were a lot of other people dressed in white coming
behind him on horses.

"I saw myself coming out of the house and falling
on my knees, and I started crying and screaming, 'Lord,
not now, not now! I'm not ready!' When I saw Jesus,
everything in me that was of the world left; it was time

to get right with God and nothing else mattered. Then Jesus opened His mouth. I never heard anything, but I saw His words start floating through the air and they destroyed everything in their path. And then I woke up and it was pitch dark and my bed was soaked with sweat and I was crying. I thought I'd lost all hope and I was already in hell.

"Then I looked across the room to the curtains, which were pulled shut, and I saw a glimmer of light in the middle. There was hope! I got up and ripped those curtains open. I've never been more thankful; I started jumping and shouting and thanking the Lord. As soon as I could get dressed, I ran down to the church and that day I made up my mind that I was going to give my life to the Lord."

When we talked, it had been more than eight years since Terry's dream, yet it was as clear to him as if he'd seen it that very hour. "As the years go by, the Lord continues to reveal more and more to me about that dream. I read in Revelation (the last book in the Bible) the vision John saw of Jesus returning to earth on a great white horse, and out of his mouth came a sword, and that sword was His Word. That's what I saw."

Terry realizes that few people have such a dramatic conversion. He doesn't know why God chose to reach him in that manner, but he knows that God "reaches you where you can be reached." He explained it with a simple illustration: "It's like a phone call. I have to call you where you are. God communicates with you in a way that reaches you. He reached me at a time when I was in transition."

That was the start of Terry's relationship with God. He didn't broadcast the news of his experience right away, but there were some obvious changes. One involved his temper — he was a "hothead" who often was thrown out of games. The other was his language — "my vocabulary consisted of four-letter words." Within a few weeks, both of those areas were brought under control. "My friends noticed the change immediately."

Other changes did not come so easily, and he admitted that the transition from a man who lives for the things of this world to one who is committed totally to Jesus Christ will last the rest of his life. "The flesh doesn't understand spiritual things," he explained. "We make a commitment to the Lord, and that's a spiritual commitment, but the flesh doesn't care. You let your guard down for a second and the flesh takes over."

Much of the intensity that once was expressed in anger was redirected into basketball. And ministry. Terry began holding a Bible study for fellow high school students and met his wife, Vonnie, through that study. With success in basketball came college scholarship offers. Of course, a man of his size and ability was a prize recruiting catch, and there were plenty of inducements to take more than what NCAA rules permitted.

Terry wasn't tempted. "I felt responsible to God for everything I did. I felt if I received something from somebody, I had to give something back in return. I didn't want to owe anyone except God."

In fact, the school he chose was one of the few that didn't actively recruit him. Initially, he decided to attend Iowa, until he sensed God leading him to stay in Chicago and attend DePaul. Though Coach Meyer hadn't contacted Cummings, he was most willing to allow the young man to heed God's direction.

Fans have a hard time believing that Terry's relationship with God is uppermost in his life. He'd quit basketball immediately if he believed God were telling him to do so. In fact, he almost did quit after his sophomore season.

Terry began to sense God's call to the ministry soon after his conversion. He didn't understand it at first, even though he was teaching Bible studies in high school and college. As the desire grew, he spent many hours in prayer: He knew God had called him into ministry, but what exactly was expected? At the end of that period, he realized that he was called to be an evangelist, and began preparing for ordination.

After his sophomore season, Terry was dissatisfied with his performance in basketball, and thought perhaps it was time to devote all of his energies to preaching. Again he went to God in prayer and learned that it wasn't time yet to give up the game that provided his public platform.

"I tell you," he said earnestly, "the relationship is so simple. When you start talking about a relationship between God and man, it's just as simple as a telephone call. 'Hello Jesus. I need your help.' And He answers, 'You got it!' " "

"How do you know you're talking to God?" I asked.

"The Scriptures teach that God inhabits the praises of His people. So through praise we are inducted into His presence. We're talking to the source. It's really that simple."

So simple that he doesn't fret when things go wrong. While Terry was in college, his son contracted spinal meningitis. "It hurt to see my boy whimpering and crying. One of his eyes was swollen shut and I started to cry. I told the Lord that He knew how much I loved my son. I was going to believe His Word. I wasn't going to get fanatical. I wasn't going to start screaming. 'I'm just going to believe You.' About two days later, my boy was totally healed. The doctors said they couldn't believe it; he should have died."

His prayers don't always have "happy" endings. During his first year in San Diego, Terry developed an irregular heartbeat — a disorder called arrhythmia — that jeopardized his career. Again he prayed, then agreed to accept an experimental new drug that would control the problem as long as he was playing basketball. The only side effect has been discoloration of patches of his skin on his thighs, arms and shoulders. He will probably stop taking the drug once he's out of pro ball.

If Terry believed God, why wasn't he healed immediately? Terry answers by going to Scripture, then making an observation about society. He relates that the Bible promises healing, but it doesn't happen apart from our faith.

"We're living in an instantaneous society," he said. "McDonald's, Burger King. We want things to happen right now. But God's not that way. The Scriptures teach us to pray without ceasing. Some people say when we pray we should get it right away. But it doesn't always happen."

Today, Terry Cummings plays basketball for eight months of each year. The rest of his time is spent preaching. He travels frequently to various cities, holding rallies and revival services. He writes and sings his own music. He gives a powerful message. Kids enjoy hearing him, for he tells them that they can succeed, and he reveals the source of true success.

His speaking style is penetrating, with frequent use of word pictures. "We're like flowers," he says in many of his messages. "If they get too much rain, they won't grow. Too much sun, and they wilt. You must have the right balance. Our lives are like that. If we experience too much good — the sunshine — then we'll suffer from the glare. But too much rain, and we'll be depressed. I believe I've experienced that balance."

Terry wants others to have that balance, too, and he knows where they can find it. It starts with the relationship. You don't need a special dream to find it.

POST-GAME WRAPUP

Keith Erickson

The Forum is nearly empty. Cars are filing out of the parking lot and heading onto the southern California freeways. Most of the car radios are tuned to the Lakers Post-Game Show with Chick Hearn and his color analyst, Keith Erickson. It's time to reflect on the game, interview one of the stars, review statistics, and catch up on scores from around the league.

Keith Erickson has complemented Hearn's famous "words-eye-view" in the broadcast booth since the 1979-80 season. He brings a rich background to his analysis. In college, he played for two national championship teams at UCLA. He was also a member of the U.S. Olympic volleyball team in 1964. During a twelve-year NBA career, Keith competed in five World Championship series and was a member of the record-setting Lakers team that won 33 straight games and the 1972 championship.

Here, then, is Keith's FAST BREAK wrapup:

Terry Cummings had a dream. A. C. Green walked forward in a church service. Butch Carter prayed in the privacy of a hotel room. Mark Eaton was guided by a counselor at a youth camp. Marques Johnson was lying in a hospital bed.

While the individual circumstances were unique, each of the basketball players in this book has, at some point in his life, made the same commitment. That commitment has to do with the person of Jesus Christ — understanding who He is, and responding to His call on their lives.

John Wooden is considered by many as the greatest basketball coach of all time. From my experience playing for him, I believe one reason he was so great was that he constantly drilled us on the fundamentals. In the next few paragraphs, I would like to give you a few fundamentals that will allow you to experience a spiritual fast break.

First, a spiritual fast break requires a transition from a life of sin.

On the basketball court, a fast break starts on defense. You cannot run the break without the ball. So the defense must pressure the offense for a steal or gain position for a rebound. As soon as it possesses the ball, it instantly reverses direction and heads up-court on offense, looking for a quick score.

The same is true spiritually. Let me use my own experience to explain. Halfway through my pro basketball career, I found myself with basically everything the world had to offer. I had all the money I could want, I was able to travel, I had many friends, and I was popular in the Los Angeles area. But none of those things made me truly happy. I recognized that I was missing something, and that I wouldn't find it by making more money, traveling more, or having more friends.

My problem was that I was going my own way apart from God. The Bible says that "all have sinned and fall short of the glory of God" (Romans 3:23). Many people think of sin only in terms of doing bad things like stealing, getting drunk, and committing murder. However, God has revealed His standard through Jesus Christ and the Bible, and by that measurement, everyone in the world falls short. My unhappiness with life was due to the fact that I was running my own life independent of God and His ways.

A spiritual fast break is a break toward fulfillment, purpose, and eternal life in Christ.

It's not enough just to gain possession of the ball; you must push the ball up-court and score. Spiritually, it's not enough to turn *from* sin; we need to turn *toward* Christ.

After I realized that something was missing in my life, I began searching for answers. I tried a lot of things, particularly in the area of cults and the occult. One after another, I found each of them was a dead-end street. They didn't provide answers to such basic questions as, "Why am I here on earth?" and "Where am I going?"

Then one day someone told me about Jesus Christ and it was like a firecracker going off in my brain. No one had ever explained to me that God created earth, that He also created me as a person, and that He had a plan by which we could know and enjoy each other. Which leads to the third fundamental.

A spiritual fast break is made possible by God's Son, Jesus Christ, who paid the price for our sins.

Of course, I had heard the name of Jesus Christ. But until a friend explained it to me, and God opened me up to understand it, I never realized that Jesus was God, that He came to earth and lived among men to show us what God was like, and that He provided the way for us to know God.

Jesus said, "I am the way, and the truth, and the life; no one comes to the Father, but through Me" (John 14:6).

The reason Jesus is the *only* way we can know God is because He lived a sinless life. Then, through His death by crucifixion He paid the penalty for our sins. Three days after His death He came back to life in the event we call the resurrection, which we celebrate on Easter Sunday. Afterward He appeared to His disciples, then to more than five hundred people at one time.

The resurrection proved that Jesus Christ was who He claimed to be, and that He has the power to unite us with God. But it's not enough just to know that. Each of us must make a decision.

A spiritual fast break can be experienced by acknowledging that you are a sinner and accepting God's gift — the payment of your sins by Jesus Christ.

Each of the men in this book chose to accept Jesus Christ's payment for their sin and allowed Him to take over control of their lives. I made a similar commitment in 1973 when through a simple prayer I admitted I was not doing things God's way and asked Him to forgive me. I invited Jesus Christ to come into my life and change me. And He did.

This is the most important part of the book, for at this moment you can experience your own spiritual fast break if you're ready. You can invite Christ into your life through prayer, which is simply talking with God. Your prayer could include the following thoughts:

1) Admit you are a sinner.
2) Thank God for sending His Son, Jesus Christ, to pay the penalty for your sin by dying on the cross and then rising from the dead.
3) Accept His forgiveness for your sins.
4) Ask Jesus Christ to come into your life and make you a new person.

Why don't you take a minute right now to pray this prayer in your own words?

*   *   *

Did you pray those thoughts to God? If you did, Jesus Christ came into your life. You may or may not feel any different at this moment. But that's not important because your prayer is based on what God promises, not on how you feel. However, if you did ask Christ to be your Lord and Savior, your life will begin to change.

There were some immediate effects on my life. For one thing, I knew that my search was finally over. I'd found my purpose for living. And some of my bad habits, particularly my foul language, began to change as a result.

But I also made the mistake of not following through right away. It was nearly two years before I started reading the Bible and attending church regularly. Only then did my life begin to grow and change significantly.

So let me make a few suggestions. Realize that God is now living in you and He expects you to obey Him by:

1. *Spending some time every day reading the Bible.* The Bible is God speaking to us. If you don't know where to start, begin by reading the Gospel of John in the New Testament.

2. *Taking time to pray every day.* Prayer is simply talking with God, just as you would talk with your best friend. You can start by thanking Jesus Christ for

touching your life. You might also ask God to teach
you His ways as you read from the Bible.

3. *Attending church.* Start going every Sunday. Many
   NBA players realize how important this is. During
   the season when games and practices are scheduled
   on Sunday, it's difficult for players to attend church.
   That's why most teams now hold chapel services. It's
   a chance for them to pray together and encourage
   each other, and to hear a message from the Bible.

Choose a church that teaches the Bible. Attending
church will give you an opportunity to meet with other
Christians, and you can encourage each other to grow
in faith. You should also get into a small group Bible
study. This will provide a chance to ask questions and
gain support as you begin living for Christ.

If you have given your life to Jesus Christ as a result
of reading this book, or if you have more questions
about the Christian life and what it means, please write.
We would like to help you become all God wants you
to be.

We'll be praying that like many NBA players, you,
too, will experience a spiritual fast break through Jesus
Christ.

For more information about knowing Jesus Christ or
growing in your faith, write to:

Al Janssen

c/o Here's Life Publishers

P.O. Box 1576

San Bernardino, CA 92402

Acknowledgments

I am especially grateful to Al Egg for his wise counsel and prayer support throughout this project.

Special thanks to the Portland Trail Blazers, and particularly publicity director John White and his assistant Jennifer Glickman, for all their courtesies offered during the 1985-86 season. They provided much valuable information, plus access to the games and players. They are true professionals.

The following NBA public relations directors also provided valuable assistance: Jeff Twiss (Boston), Tim Hallam (Chicago), Kevin Sullivan (Dallas), Harvey Kirkpatrick (Denver), Jim Foley (Houston), Scott Carmichael (L.A. Clippers), Josh Rosenfeld (L.A. Lakers), Bill King (Milwaukee), Jim Lampariello (New Jersey), John Cirillo (New York), John Lashway (Portland), Jeff Troesch (Seattle), and Bill Kreifeldt (Utah).

Thanks also to Brian McIntyre, director of public relations for the NBA, for credentials and a wealth of helpful information at the 1986 All-Star game.

A very special thanks to Denise Svendsen for transcribing nearly twenty-five hours of taped interviews.

The following materials provided background information for certain chapters of this book:

Chapter 1: Interview with Alex English, *USA Weekend*, February 7-9, 1986.

Chapter 2: "Kevin McHale: The Celtics' Working-Class Hero" by Mike Carey, *Basketball Digest*, January, 1986.

"McHale surprised a Lot of People . . . Even Auerbach" by Joe Fitzgerald, *The Boston Herald,* June 2, 1985.

"Home Court Advantages," by Mike Carey, *The Boston Herald Sunday Magazine,* October 20, 1985.

"McHale: Celtic Who Gives Rivals Fits" by Sam Goldaper, *New York Times,* May 27, 1985.

"Please don't call him Mr. McNasty" by Allene Volsin, *Los Angeles Herald Examiner,* May 14, 1985.

Chapter 3: "A.C. Green: He does it His way" by Frank Brady, *Los Angeles Herald Examiner,* September 20, 1985.

"The Greening of the Lakers: Riley's impressed" by Frank Brady, *Los Angeles Herald Examiner,* October 19, 1985.

"Journey of Discovery" by Jack McCallum and Bruce Newman, *Sports Illustrated,* February 3, 1986.

Chapter 4: Special thanks to Bill Horlacher for providing a wealth of material including a transcript of the "FCA Athletes Speak Out" program in December of 1980, transcripts of interviews with Bobby Jones and Julius Erving, plus numerous magazine articles. Thanks also to Al Egg for providing the transcript of Julius Erving's acceptance speech on behalf of Bobby Jones for the NBA Sixth Man Award.

"The Doctor Opens Up His Medicine Bag" by Pat Putnam, *Sports Illustrated,* May 17, 1976.

"Doctor J's toughest case" by Gary Hoenig, *New York Times Magazine,* February 13, 1977.

"McGinnis Trade Gives Dr. J Chance to Return" by Alex Sachare, *Los Angeles Times,* August 27, 1978.

"Sixers' Erving ponders future" by David Kahn, *The Oregonian,* Wednesday, January 1, 1986.

"Bobby Jones: Mr. Unusual" by Bill Horlacher, *Athletes in Action,* Spring 1980.

Chapter 6: "Eaton was worth the wait" by George Pohly, *Basketball Times,* May 25, 1985.

"Head and shoulders above the competition" by Dale Robertson, *Houston Post,I April 21, 1985.*

"The Great Wall dwarfs Olajuwon" by Ed Fowler, Houston Chronicle, April 20, 1985.

"Jazz's Eaton: A Tall Tale Who Blocked Out Failure" by Lex Hemphill, *Los Angeles Herald Tribune,* March 20, 1985.

"Eaton Paying Huge Dividends to Jazz" by Mike Weber, *The Sporting News,* March 4, 1985.

"The NBA isn't snickering any longer" by Dave Blackwell, *Deseret News,* February 13, 1985.

"Jazz enjoy lifestyle on Eaton's block" by Kevin O'Keeffe, *The Sunday Express News,* February 3, 1985.

Chapter 7: "Questions Arise in Marques Johnson Trade" by Sam McManis and Mike Littwin, *Los Angeles Times,* February 9, 1985.

"Straight Forward" by Don Greenburg, *The Register,* February 9, 1985.

"Marques ends his silence" by Don Greenberg, *The Register,* September 26, 1985.

"Fast Breaks for an NBA Star" by Mike Morrow, *Athletes in Action,* Winter, 1985.

Chapter 10: Special thanks to Scotty Stirling who as vice president of operations for the NBA granted permission for this special story on referee Ed Rush.

Chapter 12: "A minister with muscle" by Sean Callahan, *Sportsview,* 1984.

"The Best Out of Nothing" by Alan Steinberg, *Inside Sports,* January, 1984.

Chapter 13:   Special thanks to Keith Erickson for his contribution in this final chapter, and for his encouragement and counsel while writing this book.